Dr. O's 10 Essential Ingredients for Success©

A triumphant journey of a woman who flourishes while encountering, misogyny, illness, adolescent trauma, racism, and harassment during her lifetime. By embracing the 10 essential ingredients, Dr. Osborne was able to overcome many of life's difficulties.

Written by

Marian Osborne, Ed. D.

Copyright © 2018

Marian Osborne, Ed. D.

Bethune Publishing House, Inc.
The Bethune Group MMB

First Printing

All rights reserved, including the right

to reproduce this work in any form whatsoever without written permission from the publisher, except for brief passages in connection with a review.

Photographs may not be reproduced without permission of the owner.

For information write:
Bethune Publishing House, Inc.
P. O. Box 2008
Daytona Beach, FL 32115-2008
docbethune@tbginc.org
Phone: 386-999-0092

Cover designed by **John-Mark McLeod**

J2maginations, LLC

J2maginations@gmail.com

Book design and page layout by
Bethune Publishing House, Inc.

Printed in the United States of America

Library of Congress Control Number: 2018936089

ISBN 9781946566102

Dr. O's 10 Essential Ingredients for Success   Marian Osborne, Ed D

Dr. O's
10 Essential Ingredients for Success

To contact Dr. Marian Osborne:
www.drmarianosborne.org
Phone: 561-455-4471
drmarianosborne@comcast.net

Dr. O's 10 Essential Ingredients for Success   Marian Osborne, Ed D

Table of Contents   Page

Biography	Who is Dr. Marian Osborne?	8
Dedication	My Support System	12
Introduction	My Story	13
Ingredient 1	Faith God is ever present in times of storms.	18
Ingredient 2	Tenacity Don't quit no matter what!	22
Ingredient 3	Controlling Your Thoughts Adolescent Trauma Learn how to control your thoughts	32
Ingredient 4	Courage The Little Giant	39
Ingredient 5	Integrity	54
Ingredient 6	Humility Diagnosed with Brain Tumor	67
Ingredient 7	Know Who You Are Cultural Identity, Racism, and Institutional Trauma.	81

Table of Contents (cont.)   Page

Ingredient 8   **Be Loving**   99
A Gift from God "My Wife" (Written by Pastor Reginald C Osborne)

Ingredient 9   **Be Laser Focused**   112
What Can Be Done to Improve the Quality of Life?

Ingredient 10   **Leave a Legacy**   128
What do you want people to say about you when you are no longer here?

Dr. O's 10 Essential Ingredients for Success   Marian Osborne, Ed D

Dr. Marian Osborne
LCADC, MCAP, CMHP, ACRPS, CCS

Biography
Who is Dr. Marian Osborne?

Dr. Marian Osborne's work in the academic community has garnered her numerous awards. She is the proud recipient of the Who's Who Award-American Junior College, Student of the Month Award, recipient of two academic scholarships, and has graduated Cum Laude from New Jersey City University. In addition, she also graduated from Seton Hall University as Cum Laude. Dr. Osborne has participated in several graduate programs, including Harvard University. She served as an adjunct professor at Montclair State University, William Patterson College, and also found time in her busy schedule to provide consultation for those requesting it. She attributes all of her successes to her relationship with God and the support of a loving husband for over 50 years. Dr. Marian Osborne, one of five children, was born on September 18, 1948, in Harlem New York. She married Reginald Charles Osborne Jr. on September 30, 1967 and is the mother of two daughters: Felicia and Yvette.

Family is important to Dr. Osborne and it is evident as she proudly talks about her husband, daughters and three grandchildren. At the age of 17, Dr. Osborne graduated from high school and had aspirations of becoming a teacher. It was her faith and her early commitment to the church that enabled her to realize her dreams and accomplish a great deal in life in spite of her challenges. Dr. Osborne earned an academic scholarship from New Jersey City University where she was able to complete a Bachelor of Arts degree in education as she minored in psychology.

Her faith and knowing that she could accomplish what she set out to do enabled her to complete her Master of Arts degree in Education. Dr. Osborne received numerous awards for her commitment and dedication. After several years working as an educator, Dr. Osborne decided to complete a rigorous doctoral program at Seton Hall University in May of 1999 a true professional in the academia world and an excellent role model for women are a few of the qualities describing her.

She has served as a public-school teacher, and also an elementary school principal. Dr. Osborne was the only female of African descent to hold the title of County Supervisor of Child Study in the New Jersey State Department of Education from 1992-1995. It was during her tenure at the New Jersey State Department of Education that she coordinated all special education programs and services in Passaic County to ensure compliance with federal and state rules and regulations. It was during this time that Osborne participated in the implementation of state monitoring of school districts to ensure compliance in the areas of pupil performance, curriculum core course proficiencies, certification, facilities standards and mandated programs.

As Director of Special Services for the third largest school district in New Jersey, Dr. Osborne provided viable information and training to educators as they engaged challenging students with the necessary skills needed to be successful. Dr. Osborne also served as president of the Passaic County Association of Special Education Administrators. This was the period in time leadership and guidance was provided to all the special education directors in Passaic County.

It was Dr. Osborne's challenging experiences that lead her to become passionate about working with victims of trauma and other behavior health disorders. She currently holds the following certifications and licenses: Licensed Clinical Alcohol Drug Counselor, Master's Level Certified Addiction Professional, Certified Clinical Supervisor, Advanced Certified Relapse Prevention Specialist and Certified Mental Health Professional.

Dedication

First to God, then Reggie, Felicia, Yvette, Earl, Jasmine, Earl Jr., and especially my precious princess Sydney Tankard - without their unconditional love and support this book would never have been completed. I also would like to dedicate this book in memory of my dear friend Carol Neely Blowe who departed this life January 1, 2017. She was my colleague and friend who I will always be indebted to. I also would like to dedicate this book to my brother Philip A. Crew who departed this life August 13, 2017. He was the best brother a sister could ever have.

Much love for my brother-in-law Maurice Oliver Osborne who departed this life July 29, 2017.

Introduction
My Story

I want to share with you my story about a triumphant journey and how I managed to flourish while encountering illness, adolescent trauma, racism, and harassment during my lifetime. An estimated 223,400,000 individuals will suffer at least one traumatic event in their life time. (National Institute of Mental Health in Bethesda, MD) Unfortunately, too often we don't know what to do when the challenges in life cross our path.

This book will provide practices that will benefit anyone experiencing traumatic events in their life. As an author, my desire is to reveal some of my personal struggles and how I have learned these 10 ingredients that have worked for me over time. I am confident that anyone can gain strength and healing while recovering from almost any situation. After all, I did.

What are some difficulties women experience in a negative and sometimes hostile environment? How are individual lives impacted as a result of traumatic experiences? There are definitely different types of trauma. This book will provide the reader with several types of sudden unanticipated trauma (cultural, identity, trauma caused by racism, and institutional trauma) experienced by the writer and how these experiences have impacted her life as she regained her confidence and control and continued to soar.

Often traumatic experiences typically do not result in long-term impairment for most people. It needs to be understood that it is normal to experience some traumatic events across a lifespan; It has been noted that frequently individuals, families, and communities respond to them with resilience. Unfortunately, it has been proven that children and adolescents are much more likely than adults to develop trauma-related disorders, especially when trauma is repeated, and no relief or support is available.

Understanding that traumatic events can happen to anyone, there are certain risk factors that impact some individuals greater than others. These individuals are more likely to experience a certain mentality related to the trauma following a disturbing event. Dealing with emotional and psychological trauma is the result of extraordinarily stressful events that can shatter a person's sense of security, making an individual feel helpless while they are in a dangerous environment. Traumatic experiences often involve a threat to life or safety, but any situation that leaves you feeling over whelmed and isolated can be traumatic, even if it doesn't involve physical harm. Often, it's not the objective facts that determine whether an event is traumatic, but a person's subjective emotional experience of the event. The more frightened and helpless a person feels, the more likely they are impacted.

Having grown up in the 60's and 70's, during the height of the civil rights era, I experienced ongoing, relentless stress during my adolescent years in high school. I was fortunate to have had a spiritual experience that gave me the strength and fortitude to rise above these experiences. The blessing was realizing early in my life that a person can't run from everything that's difficult in life or expect instant results simply because you have faith. Often life challenges can stretch you and enlarge your horizons. I recognized that as a child of Faith, I had the power within me to overcome any difficulty – which included everything in the world and everything the world brought my way.

When difficulty came my way, through fear, sickness, worry, financial mishaps, racism, I just put my faith to work by quoting the Word of God. "...for every one born of God overcomes the world. This is the victory that has overcome the world, even our faith." (1 John 5:4 NIV) Some research suggests that when children or adolescents experience a traumatic event in their early years, they are most likely to be traumatized. The events that occurred during my adolescent years were unexpected and I had little preparation. Consequently, it caused me to feel powerless as it was repeated throughout my years in high school and throughout my adult life.

The events that occurred definitely interrupted a sense of safety. I was fortunate that I was able to stay grounded while finding spirituality and support from within and also from people outside of my family environment.

As I reflect back over my life, I realized that certain ingredients contributed to my successes in life. Reflection is not always easy but in order to write this book, it was necessary. I felt compelled to write about these experiences and share how I was able to raise above all the difficulties life brought my way. By using these 10 ingredients I was able to reach my dreams and experience joyful success in life.

Ingredient 1

Faith

Knowing God is ever present in times of storms

What is faith to me? Faith to me doesn't deny the circumstance but faith denies the right of that circumstance to control me. There are difficulties in life we all must and will encounter *(divorce, abuse, separation, death of loved one, financial ruin, addictions, poverty, incarceration, unemployment, inadequate education, violence, civil unrest, homelessness, sickness, Hopelessness, and racism)*, but we must be determined not to allow these difficulties to control our destiny.

I was up early this morning as I am every morning on work days. I was prepared to leave home for another day at the Board of Education as a central office administrator. This particular public school is a State controlled school district. The state took this school over as a result of poor performance by students and the misuse of funds by administrators. I was hired to work in this district after leaving a position at the New Jersey State Department of Education.

Dr. O's 10 Essential Ingredients for Success   Marian Osborne, Ed D

I was feeling quite tranquil that very morning as I ran my bath water while brushing my teeth. I began to sing an old church song I often heard my mother sing many times before. *"This world is not my home, I am just passing by, my treasures and my hopes – they all are up on high, my family and my friends, they all have gone before, And I cannot feel at home in this world anymore"* My mom had since gone home to be with the Lord and I was reminiscing about her this particular morning. She was a woman who had dedicated her life to the work of God and encouraged all of her children to always do the best you can, and God would bless your efforts.

I kissed my husband good-by as I left out of the door for work. As I arrived at my usual time of 7:25 am, my secretary Maria was having her usual coffee and roll outside of my office door. I stopped and said good morning as I entered my office. It was a pleasant thought to know that Maria my secretary was always prompt and efficient. She never took off from work but was extremely dedicated to her job. (She had been the secretary for all of the department directors for over 30 years and therefore she was very knowledgeable) I was also proud of the fact that I was the first woman of color to hold the Central Office position of Special Education Director in such a large school district. I was very committed to making a difference for the students there.

Approximately at 8:45 am I received a phone call from the superintendent's office (Chief School Administrator and my supervisor) requesting my presence. This was a very unusual request that was made by the superintendent so early in the morning. I realized I was not his choice for the current position I held as the Director of Special Services. It was unfortunate for this superintendent that I was already hired prior to his tenure in this school district.

When I entered the superintendent's office, he appeared to be nervous and agitated. He handed me a letter signed by him indicating that I was under investigation by the state and that two gentlemen (special investigators from the New Jersey State Department of Education) would be coming to my office within fifteen minutes to question me. The letter also indicated that I was to give over to these special investigators all requested documents that include department expenditures for the past five years. (My yearly budget was no less than forty million dollars.) I was also directed to submit my department's attendance record book which everyone in my department (including myself) signed on a daily basis. I asked the superintendent "Why am I being investigated?" He looked at me and then looked down but did not give me an answer. He turned and dismissed me. I went back to my office very perplexed and began to collect the information I was directed to give to the two male investigators from the New Jersey State Department of Education.

I realize that discouragement is the number one reason people give up. I am so grateful that I have seeds of faith that has been planted inside me that gives me hope when discouragement comes my way. *Hebrews 10:35 (NIV)* says *"Do not cast away your confidence for it will be richly rewarded."* I know how important it is for me to meditate on God's promises and live a life that is pleasing and honoring to Him. God has always been faithful to me in the past-no matter what the circumstances looked like. I knew that morning my faith was being tested.

One of the main ingredients that propelled my success in life was my faith in God. By including the ingredient faith in every aspect of my life, I was able to face my greatest fears. I found that this ingredient by far is the most important one in my life and it works every time.

Ingredient 2

Tenacity

Don't Quit No Matter What!

I asked my secretary if she would begin to gather the requested information and I indicated to her that I would be receiving two investigators from the state department of education that morning. Within 15 minutes of returning to my office from the superintendent's office, the gentlemen arrived. It was explained to me by the investigators that the superintendent was alleging that I had stolen books, money and conducted myself inappropriately in my position as director. Looking back in retrospect, I realized that I was being falsely accused without any documentation to sustain any claim.

At the back of my office I had a conference room where I would conduct meetings. When the gentlemen arrived, we met in that room. I asked the investigators why I was being investigated. They responded that the superintendent had generated a letter with a list of undocumented infractions that I had done, and they were merely there to ask me about those infractions. As the investigators presented the information to me on a list,

I realized that the majority of the items on the list centered on the misuse of state funds. (*Since this school district was state controlled, any misappropriations would involve the state of New Jersey).* The investigators indicated that they would be reviewing all of my department's requisitions signed by me. I was very relaxed knowing that these charges were false. When the investigators left me, they indicated that they would be meeting with the business administrator to review my requisitions.

Although I was honest in all of my purchasing in the district - I had the responsibility for over 400 staff members who sent hundreds of requisitions to my office daily to be signed. There were over 200 special education teachers, 180 plus child study team members which included social workers, speech teachers, learning disability teacher consultants, psychologists, eleven secretaries, and four supervisors. It was part of my responsibility to sign off on all requisitions in my department. I was confident that I had reviewed each requisition carefully before signing. A large part of my staff was responsible for evaluating students while the rest were support staff and teachers. There were students being recommended to attend schools out of district because of the severity of their disability. These were private specialized school that required payment. Within a month's time my department generated over 600 requisitions that needed to be signed by me personally. There were times I could not justify a staff member's honesty in their purchasing of furniture, supplies, evaluation kits, trips, and more. Therefore, I would not sign off on them. Regardless if a staff member was honest or not, I was the one directly responsible for every requisition generated from my department.

It was at that moment I realized that my faith was greater than any situation I could ever encounter. I began to hum a song in my heart as I went back to my office. I quoted *"No weapon that is formed against me shall prosper"* (Isaiah 54:17 KJV). I then began to feel a peace come over me. *"For God has not given us the spirit of fear but of power, and of love, and of a sound mind. (Romans 8:31KJV)* As I continued to go over the list of items that were presented to me by the investigators, I realized that everything that was on that list was inaccurate. I remember one item in particular on that list which alleged that I had used the district's money to purchase books for my personal school advancement. I attended Seton Hall University (1997-1999) in order to meet the requirements for a doctoral degree in administration. I knew I had never ordered any personal books for school because all of my books were purchased by Seton Hall for that cohort and given out to each doctoral candidate. (Books were included in the tuition cost). It was apparent to me that this superintendent was trying to destroy my reputation or worse. I realized that he wanted to intimidate, defame, harass, and eventually have me fired.

This particular superintendent did not hire me, as I was hired by the previous superintendent who had left the district. This current superintendent was new to the district and looking back in retrospect it appeared as if he wanted to bring in his own team of directors and central office administrators into his cabinet. In addition, he wanted me to illegally classify children and place them in special education classes even though they were not eligible.

Placing special education children who have some form of a disability into general education classrooms with their neighborhood peers was the focus of the federal and state law since 1954. The Supreme Court concluded after the observance of Brown v Board of Education, that, separate…facilities are inherently unequal." Brown became the springboard upon which parents of children with disabilities in

Washington DC and Pennsylvania fought in court to end the exclusion of their children from their public schools and led directly to the passage of Public Law 94-142 in 1975. It is now known as the Individuals with Disabilities Education Act (IDEA). The education of children with disabilities with non-disabled peers was a principal objective of Congress in passing IDEA. The law entitles every eligible child with a disability to an appropriate education in the least restrictive environment with the term "restrictive" used as a measure of the child's opportunity to be educated with non-disabled peers.

This law ensures the inclusion of children with disabilities participation into general education classrooms. Special classes or separate schooling should only take place when their education could not be achieved satisfactorily in general education classrooms with the use of supplementary supports and services. In order to prevent removal for other than educational reasons, the federal law further prohibits removal based upon the category of the disabling condition, the availability of space, staff, or services, administrative convenience, or any perceived attitude of non-disabled peers or teachers.

(In this school district if children in special education take the state test, their examination scores would not count against the district's overall test scores. Their test results would be disaggregated or separated from the

rest of the district's results. By the superintendent ordering my staff to classify students into special education (who were not eligible) whose test results were low in general education, it would automatically raise the district test scores and the superintendent would be hailed for improving a failing district. It would indicate that the district had improved but in reality, they only moved students from general education classes into special education so that their scores did not impact the overall district scores. The superintendent instructed my staff to disregard the law and put these students into special education even though they were not eligible.)

I communicated to my staff and those responsible for assessing students to follow and obey the law. I gave my staff that directive, I was persecuted continuously. The consequences of me taking a stand and following the federal and state regulations, I was harassed continually by the superintendent for over five years. I felt so alone those years as my standing up for what I felt was the right thing to do for children seem to go unnoticed. Unfortunately, my efforts to obey the law were ineffective because the district placed an inordinate number of students during those five years into special education. (see chart on page 30).

I was fortunate that I did have tenure, so unless the superintendent could demonstrate or prove that I had continuous poor performance, conducted myself in a manner that was unacceptable or prove that I was responsible for the misuse of district funds, it would be almost impossible for him to remove me from my current position as director of special services. Although I was allowed to remain on my job, at times I became isolated and ostracized.

The following morning after the investigators left, the business administrator paid me a visit. He was shaking his head in dismay as he mumbled, "I told them every requisition from your office was appropriate." He conveyed to me that the investigators went through over 600 requisitions and could not find one error. I thanked him for letting me know, but I knew my faith in God sustained me through that entire encounter. Although that particular situation might seem to be over, I received continuous harassment from this superintendent. Only my faith kept me sane and gave me a strong desire to hold on. I was able to keep a song in my heart. After having three years of stellar evaluations, the superintendent began to give me average performance evaluations. He also submitted a recommendation suggesting that I do not get a raise, but his suggestion did not stand. It seemed that everything which he tried to do to me did not stand. The weapon was formed but it did not prosper.

Unfortunately, the harassment continued. While conducting a parent meeting one evening, the superintendent and a board member ordered my car to be towed from my personal parking space which had my name on it. When I left my parent meeting I had no way of getting home in a dangerously inner-city area at night. There had been numerous acts of harassment, but I was able through my faith in God endure every situation. My husband and I made a decision to secure an attorney to fight our battles. Thank God, we were able to prevail at the end, but I learned that having stamina in my everyday life is essential in order to be successful. The ingredient of tenacity taught me that I must never give up. I did eventually receive a letter and report from the New Jersey State Department of Education vindicating me on all alleged infractions. (See page 31)

Dr. O's 10 Essential Ingredients for Success   Marian Osborne, Ed D

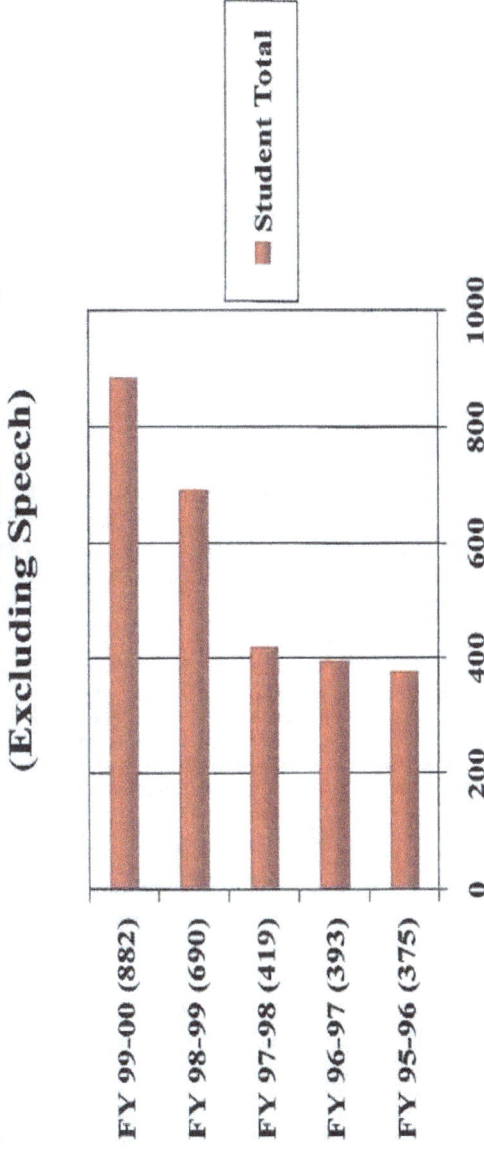

Dr. O's 10 Essential Ingredients for Success   Marian Osborne, Ed D

State of New Jersey
DEPARTMENT OF EDUCATION
PO Box 500
TRENTON, NJ 08625-0500

DONALD T. DIFRANCESCO
Acting Governor

VITO A. GAGLIARDI, SR.
Commissioner

March 30, 2001

Dr. Marian Osborne
Director of Special Services
State-Operated School District
▇▇▇▇
33-35 Church Street
▇▇▇▇, New Jersey 07505-1306

Dear Dr. Osborne:

       Your letter of March 12, 2001 addressed to the New Jersey State Board of Education has been referred to me for a response. You have asked why the Department of Education conducted an investigation concerning you and have requested a copy of any final report on that investigation. In addition, I note that your attorney, Matthew A. Sumner, Esq., has requested a copy of the report pursuant to the Right to Know Law. We appreciate your interest in this matter and thank you for writing.

       Enclosed please find a copy of a report prepared by the Investigation Unit of the department's Office of Compliance Investigation, entitled "Investigation Report - February 2001: State-Operated School District of ▇▇▇▇ Dr. Marian Osborne - Various Allegations." As stated in the report, that investigation was conducted as a result of information provided by district officials to the department about allegations concerning you. As the report also states, "As a result of the investigation, the allegations could not be substantiated."

       I hope that this information is helpful to you and wish you well.

Sincerely,

Madeleine W. Mansier

Madeleine W. Mansier
Chief of Staff

Z:\SOSD\MWM:mg\Osborne-Invest
Enclosure
c: Maud Dahme
     Vito A. Gagliardi, Sr.

2001 APR 4 PM 2 58

www.state.nj.us/education

New Jersey Is An Equal Opportunity Employer • Printed on Recycled and Recyclable Paper

Ingredients 3

Controlling Your Thoughts

Adolescent Trauma

On September 18, 1948, I, Marian Crew (Osborne) was born to Hallie and Murray Crew at Harlem Hospital in New York City. Life was good for Hallie and Murray as they were destined to provide a happy home and life for me and my two siblings. Eventually, my parents had two other children-one that was 1 year younger and another 10 years younger. My father was an entrepreneur at an early age. He provided for his family and also other families in the neighborhood who might not have been as fortunate as the Crew family.

I remember my father during Christmas time. He had purchased crates of fruit and began giving out food to other children and families in our neighborhood in Brooklyn New York. Murray (father) worked for the New York City housing authorities and also owned several businesses and houses.

In Harlem my father owned a barber shop and a beauty parlor which my mother worked as a licensed beautician. Both parents worked hard to provide for their 5 children. I remember going to the refrigerator and had plenty of food to eat. Our Christmases were fabulous! We received anything we asked for and more. There were so many toys, candy and fruit spread all over the entire floor near the tree on Christmas day. When we went to school, we were always well dressed and our mother (the beautician) kept our hair always looking fresh and neat. My mom really enjoyed working and providing for her children. My father was my mother's second marriage. She was married when she was younger and never had children from her previous marriage.

My School Years

My elementary school *teacher* in the sixth grade at P.S. 26 in Brooklyn New York was Mr. Huntly. Mr. Huntly demonstrated to the class that he really cared for each student and worked hard to ensure that they did well academically. When we would go to lunch or recess and got reported by the monitor, Mr. Huntly would reprimand us by striking us on our hand with the ruler. He also rewarded us when we complied with other school staff and demonstrated good behavior. Although he used corporal punishment to discipline us, (which is not permitted in schools today) he communicated to his students that he really cared about them. He was such an inspiration to me in my early years.

During my junior high school years, I had so much fun. I recall that each year we would put on a play, usually a musical that was so exciting to all the students. One year we performed South Pacific, another year the *King and I,* and we also performed *The Sound of Music.* Junior high school was a great experience for me in many ways. (In Brooklyn, junior high school included 7th, 8th and 9th grades). It was during those years that I really felt I had accomplished so much in school. In the state of New York, every student had to complete a Regents examination in different subjects (state test) in order to graduate. This was one of the requirements for all students before exiting junior high school and moving on to senior high school.

It was in the ninth grade (junior high school) that I received the highest Regents examination grade of 98 in Algebra in the entire school. When I walked through the halls, the teachers were whispering how smart I was in math. I had a great understanding of math concepts because I had a great teacher. My math teacher in the ninth grade was Mr. Dudley. He was phenomenal. As a teacher, he was able to teach the students concepts that we could understand and apply, and I do believe that contributed greatly to me achieving such a high-grade on the Regents state test that year.

As a result of my junior high grades on the state test, I graduated with honors from Nathan Hale Junior High school and entered John Jay High school math honors class. John Jay High School was considered an academic high school in Brooklyn, New York. (Some schools in New York focused on specific themes or specialties. For example, there was a school for nursing, fashion, art and design, music and technology. I chose an academic high school.) This transition for me was very difficult because it was the beginning of my traumatic experiences as a young adolescent. I knew that having a spiritual relationship and learning how to control my thoughts would be key in making it through high school.

It was during the early 1960's where there was a great deal of unrest as a result of the civil rights movement. I can remember my high school experience very vividly. My math teacher of European descent made disparaging jokes about the black students who were mandated to attend John Jay High School as a result of this federal law. My honors math teacher told jokes every day to the class even though there were only two black students in the entire class which included me. I remember the teacher told a story about taking his son on the subway train in Brooklyn. He said his son asked him "dad is that a chocolate covered man sitting over there?" The teacher stated that his son started laughing. I also remember another time he described black people's hair as looking like steel wool. I remember that there were fights between the white students and the black students (mostly boys) almost every day.

It seemed that there was such resentment that students of color were mandated to attend their white schools in the Bay Ridge section of Brooklyn. The teachers and the students communicated to the black students very clearly through their words and their actions that they did not want us at their school. There were many days I came home crying, upset, and stressed. I hated going to school. Although my earlier teachers in elementary and junior high school felt I was a smart student, I was made to feel inadequate by my teacher's comments. At first, I felt discouraged about learning and began to entertain negative thoughts.

When I look back at my high school experience, I can feel tears welling up in my eyes. I find it very difficult to write about my experiences in high school because of the pain from all those times during my adolescent school years. As a therapist, I know that pain shared is pain lessened. I remember a young black female student in my class named Yvonne who also traveled to attend this all white high school. She and I would have conversations about the unfair treatment we both experienced. I guess she didn't have the strength she needed because she tried to commit suicide by jumping off the school building that year. Although she did survive, (Yvonne was caught by responders, saving her life) she managed to make the front page of the Daily News the next day. My thinking became tarnished and very negative. After weeks into the school year, I realized that I needed to change my thinking when faced with difficult situations. If I hadn't begun to push negative thoughts out of my head and lean on God's word, I would not have made it another day or even another minute.

    I am so grateful that eventually I pushed negative thoughts away and was able to find a sense of peace during those days. Another time I witnessed a group of white boys jumping on one black student at the train station and stomping on his head with their feet fiercely. The black girls started talking and thinking that perhaps we needed to bring pieces of glass for protection in case we were attacked.

It was during my high school years that I became very discouraged and began to think that I wasn't as smart as the other students at that school. My self-esteem was being negatively impacted as a result of these high school experiences. Although my physical needs were met (food, shelter etc.) my educational, emotional, and social needs were ignored. I realize now, as a therapist, that although emotional and psychological neglect are less easy to spot, they are no less damaging to a child.

Although these events were unanticipated and unexpected, they did help shape my determination to rise above the residual effects it had on my person. It was unfortunate that I was mandated by the federal and state government to attend a high school outside of my neighborhood school district. This mandate changed my life forever. I often wonder if anyone thought about the emotional consequences to those of us who were affected by this decision? As a young black teenager, I was traumatized during my high school years and was only able to survive or bounce back because I learned to control my thinking. My parents always validated my siblings and me. They constantly told us we were beautifully made by God. They told us we were smart and destined for greatness. I always believed them. What about the ones of us who did not have that validation?

My spiritual experiences also saved my life and I am so grateful. Accepting Christ as my personal Savior during my teenage years gave me a different perspective on life. It gave me the strength I needed to endure the tumultuous and racist experiences during my high school years. It was unfortunate that I didn't have many opportunities to let someone know what my daily life was like at John Jay High School. I was grateful that my faith in God and my belief in the bible opened up a whole new life for me. *"The Lord shall fight for you, and ye shall hold your peace."* (Exodus 14:14 KJV) I read that *"no weapon that was formed against me would prosper". (Isaiah 54:17 KJV) I read "if God be for us, who can be against us".* (Roman 8:31KJV)

My life changed dramatically when I changed my thinking and focus. I'm glad that I learned the importance of controlling my thoughts. I began to identify everyday those situations that triggered negative thoughts in my head. I also am able to point to my strengths (the word of God) By listing in my head the good and not-so-good ways of coping with stressful situations, I was able to increase my awareness of what really works for me. My personal experience was that when I began to choose my thoughts, it had an impact on my mood, behavior, and eventually on my decisions. I realized that, no matter how much I wanted to have a good attitude, sometimes negative thoughts would come to mind if I didn't make a different choice. I learned that thoughts go into feelings and feelings into actions and they are so related. I also learned that if I didn't learn to control my thoughts from the beginning, it would definitely affect my mood. I learned that if I wanted to be in a good mood on a regular basis, I had to start choosing to think about things that generate good feelings instead of bad ones.

I believed that God is for me and desires good things for my life. I made a choice to agree with God's word. I also made a choice to focus on the fact that I can do all things with the help of a higher power. My faith in God caused Him to show up and work supernaturally in my life! My faith helped me go to new levels of victory and I was able to rise above the negativity and to be the champion God called me to be in spite of my difficult circumstances. One of my favorite scriptures, that I carry in my heart each day, is: *"I can do all things through Christ which strengthens me." (*Philippians 4:13. KJV)

It did not matter what the teachers said about me, or how students described me, or even the difficulties life brought my way, my life was in God's hand. I believed He had great things in store for me. I began to believe that I was destined to be great in this life while I was still in school. I began to understand that how I think about myself determines the direction and the quality of life I will experience in the future.

Ingredient 4

Courage

My Introduction to "Reggie"

Being deeply loved by someone gives you strength, while loving someone deeply gives you courage. I met Reginald C. Osborne Jr. during a youth symposium at the age of 17 years old. It was at the Deliverance Evangelistic Center in Brooklyn New York. I was Reggie's partner as we both facilitated a youth program at our church. The entire congregation marched around the church to give an offering- at that time I did notice him briefly but never thought anything else. When Reggie walked in front of the 500-voice choir, the girls next to me would say "wow" he's so handsome. I was so focused at that time on serving God and living a life pleasing to Him, that I did not pay much attention to the young men in the church during my early teenage years. I wanted nothing more than to experience the peace of God in my life while encountering those high school experiences. I needed Him to remove the pain I was experiencing in my daily life. After surrendering my life to Christ, I did experience an inner peace and contentment. I became alive again and knew that I wanted to dedicate my life to doing God's service. I wanted to work in a field that helps people, perhaps become a missionary.

While working with Reggie on the youth program at my church, he eventually asked me out to lunch. Our first lunch date was at Junior's restaurant on Flatbush Avenue in Brooklyn New York. Reggie appeared to be somewhat nervous. During our lunch date, he accidentally knocked a strawberry ice cream soda in my lap. Although he was apologetic, I decided that I did not want to continue seeing him. He just seemed to be a little too clumsy for me even though he did appear to be a very nice guy. Reggie's conversations were only about his new church experience.

He was so excited about what God had done for him he did not talk about his job, family, or anything else. Looking back today, I realize now how important that was for him at that time because he had a different family up bringing than what I had experienced. Reggie's family life was not one that included going to church each Sunday. It appeared that his life was the opposite of mine. Reggie would describe his life as hanging out with the boys and smoking marijuana at home with his family. He describes his family as having a serious problem with drug usage. When he was a teenager he always thought getting high wasn't so bad. He eventually changed his thinking when several of his family members became addicted to drugs.

During the holidays and weekends at his house, individuals got high. There was a special room at his home designated for getting high. Now that he has had a spiritual experience, he was so grateful for learning about the teachings in the bible-and how putting his trust and his life in the hands of God made his life better. Reggie had so much excitement about his newly found spirituality. He was encouraged to know that many of his family members have made a change for the better. He is always willing to share this new experience he had with others. He wants to let others know that what God has done for him – He can also do for anyone who makes a decision to trust God.

As Reggie and I continued to see each other, I realized he was four years older than me and had already graduated high school and had a job working for Domino Sugar Company. Reggie worked as a research and development technician and made a pretty decent salary. I gradually became very fond of him and began to fall in love. After I graduated (1966) high school, I worked for my church as a receptionist and typist. During my lunch time, Reggie would take the bus (quit a distance) just to spend a few minutes with me during his lunch hour. I found him to be a very kind person. We spent more and more time together and eventually realized we could not live without each other. On September 30, 1967, we decided to get married. Although my father was able to pay for my wedding, he felt spending a lot of money on a wedding was wasteful and didn't make sense. He felt that people spend more time on a wedding and not on the marriage. His only concern was that Reggie had a job and was able to take care of his daughter. I love my father, but I wanted to experience and have a beautiful wedding at the age of 19.

I am grateful that my pastor and my employer at that time assisted me by providing financial support for my wedding. At that time, my dad, Murray, (biological father), was very sick with lung cancer and was in and out of the hospital constantly. Although he gave me away at my wedding, (September 30, 1967) it was quite challenging for him. He eventually passed away November of 1968. I gave birth to his first grandchild (Felicia) on September 5th, 1968 and he was able to see a picture of her before he departed this life in November of that year. I'm grateful to have had my father in my life for 19 years. He definitely encouraged his children to stay in school and be generous towards others.

My father led by example. He definitely indicated that he did not want his daughters to get pregnant before getting married. He called it *"cutting a hog"*. He communicated this to his four daughters regularly that he would be very disappointed if they became pregnant before marriage. Having that conversation with his daughters was very important. I personally did not want to disappoint my parents. I wanted them to be proud of me. I believe these conversations are important for parents to have with their children.

The Little Giant

Felicia Osborne (first born) was born September 5th, 1968 and she was such a beautiful pleasant baby. I was so pleased to bring her home from the hospital and begin my life as a new mother. After two weeks of Felicia being home, and while I was bathing her she began to scream uncontrollably. While she was screaming, she only moved one of her arms in the air. I rushed Felicia to the emergency room at Brooklyn hospital and it was determined that her left arm was broken. Because she was a newborn, (two weeks old) they admitted her to the hospital while they looked at me suspiciously. As a new mother I felt so alone and sadden by Felicia's apparent pain and being separated from my first new born baby.

After communicating with Reggie, I became aware that he had a very rare bone condition called osteogenesis imperfecta. My husband kept this from me and others because he was ashamed of his condition. Growing up he was constantly breaking bones especially his right femur (thigh bone). I was able to communicate to the hospital staff my husband's inherent condition. The orthopedic doctor was somewhat familiar with this condition and after evaluating Felicia it was determined that Felicia also had osteogenesis imperfecta. (Soft bones) This was the beginning of my life with the constant breaking of my daughter's bones as she grew up. There were times I had aspirations of going to work to help with the medical expenses, but I did not trust Felicia's care just to anyone. Felicia was very fragile and needed constant attention. Felicia exhibited such bravery while facing the possibility of fracturing a bone each day.

The next time Felicia fractured a bone was when she just started walking at 1 year of age. Felicia was excited about walking and she fell as babies do when attempting to walk. She let out such a scream that it was so piercing to anyone's ears. She had broken the largest bone in her body. We rushed Felicia to the hospital. After they had x-rayed her, it was discovered that she had a broken femur. The doctor in the emergency room asked us how she broke her leg. We responded that she was walking and fell but she has a bone condition. The emergency room doctor did not know about *osteogenesis imperfecta*. He reached for the medical book in order to gain an understanding of her condition and to find the best options for treating Felicia. I realized, at that moment in the emergency room, that I desperately needed to educate myself as her mother so that Felicia would receive the best care.

I began to study the long-term effects of this bone condition and began learning how it impacts on individual lives. Felicia spent many hours, days, and sometimes months in the hospital. We would visit her daily at the hospital but when it was time for us to leave, she began to be very sad. At times she would cry begging us not to leave her. This really broke my heart as her mother.

Osteogenesis Imperfecta

Osteogenesis imperfecta (OI) is a genetic disorder characterized by bones that break easily, often from little or no apparent cause. A classification system of different types of OI is commonly used to help describe how severely a person with OI is affected. A person may have just a few or as many as several hundred fractures in a lifetime. (Osteogenesis Imperfecta OI Foundation website). While researching this condition, I learned that there were several levels of severity of this condition. Felicia was fortunate that she could still lead a normal life with a few accommodations because of her level of the disease.

Type **I of OI** is the mildest form of the condition. People who have type I - OI have bone fractures during childhood and adolescence often due to minor trauma. When these individuals reach adulthood, they have fewer fractures. **Type II OI** is the most severe form of OI. Infants with type II have bones that appear bent or crumpled and fractured before birth. Their chest is narrow, and they have fractured and misshapen ribs and underdeveloped lungs. These infants have short, bowed arms and legs; hips that turn outward; and unusually soft skull bones.

Most infants with type II OI are stillborn or die shortly after birth, usually from breathing failure. **Type III OI** also has relatively severe signs and symptoms. Infants with OI type III have very soft and fragile bones that may begin to fracture before birth or in early infancy. Some infants have rib fractures that can cause life-threatening problems with breathing. Bone abnormalities tend to get worse over time and often interfere with the ability to walk. **Type IV OI** is the most variable form OI. Symptoms of OI type IV can range from mild to severe.

About 25 percent of infants with OI type IV are born with bone fractures. Others may not have broken bones until later in childhood or adulthood. Infants with OI type IV have leg bones that are bowed at birth but bowing usually lessens as they get older. Some types of OI are also associated with progressive hearing loss, a blue or grey tint to the part of the eye that is usually white (the sclera), teeth problems (osteogenesis imperfecta), abnormal curvature of the spine (scoliosis) and loose joints. People with this condition may have other bone abnormalities and are often shorter in stature than average.) Felicia has type IV of OI.

Challenges and Courage

I decided to take college classes while Felicia attended West Lake specialized hospital school during the day. I had a desire to specialize in the area of special education so that I would have knowledge of my daughter's rights as she ventured through her school years. I read everything I could get a hold of about children with special needs. I wanted Felicia to benefit from state and federal laws that govern programs for children with special needs. Looking back at those years, they were very challenging for me. Family members were hesitant to babysit Felicia because of her condition. One time my mom kept Felicia overnight and she fell off the bed and fractured her leg. My mother was so distraught that she said she would not be able to watch Felicia anymore. She said her nerves were bad. Thank God for my mother-in-law Dorothy. Dorothy (Reggie's mother) was the one who had an understanding about Felicia's bone condition. She was empathetic towards me and assured me that she would be willing to help me with Felicia at any time. She had raised my husband and had dealt with his constant breaking of his bones growing up. As a young mother, I was so grateful for her support and understanding.

Our medical bills were mounting because of Felicia's constant visits to the hospital and doctor. After so many breaks and constantly going back and forth to the hospital and Felicia's doctor's office, Reggie and I became overwhelmed. We had accumulated so many medical bills. Felicia's orthopedic doctor, Dr. Hansen, stated that we did not owe him anything else. He realized we were overwhelmed as a young couple with medical bills and he made a decision to give us some relief. We were so grateful and relieved that he considered our circumstances.

Every time we thought Felicia was making progress, she would break another bone. Through every situation, Felicia exhibited so much courage. She had to endure multiple surgeries during her early years. As a result of her constant breakage, her bones would curve severely. The doctors decided that they needed to break her femur in several places and insert a metal rod to provide support and avoid future breakage. That surgery was extremely painful for Felicia. After the doctor had broken her femur in several places during surgery, they had to place her in traction. This entailed pulling her already broken leg with a weight in order for her femur to grow straight. She was not sedated at that time after surgery when they stretched her leg.

It was so painful for me; I had to remove myself from the room during that procedure. My husband remained but he felt such a sense of responsibility for Felicia's condition. It pained him to see his daughter suffering with the same genetic condition he grew up with. When Felicia was two and half years old, I gave birth to her sister Yvette. During my pregnancy with Yvette I was constantly worried that she also would have this bone condition. I am so grateful that she didn't. After Yvette was born, I continued my research to determine how I could best provide Felicia with the help she needed as she matured.

It was during a time in our history that there were new laws that protected children and adults with disabilities. I was able to help my daughter (Felicia) make choices for her life and have the tools to fight for all the things she deserved. I remember after Felicia had spent most of her elementary school years (up to 4th grade) at West Lake specialized hospital school, my husband and I decided to pursue a neighborhood school in the town we lived in (Montclair). *(It was during that time that children with disabilities could be mainstreamed to schools in their neighborhood in addition to attending a general education classroom).*

After paperwork had been completed, (transferring Felicia from a specialized hospital school far from home) Felicia was picked up by her special school bus with a personal aide and brought to her neighborhood school in Montclair New Jersey. At that time Felicia used a wheel chair and she was so excited about attending a general education school just like her sister Yvette. When Felicia arrived at Northeast School in Montclair, she was met by the principal. The principal stated to Felicia that she could not attend her school because the other children would be in danger of her wheel chair. Although federal and state laws clearly stated that Felicia had a right to attend, she spent her entire first day at school sitting in the school office as directed by the principal. When Felicia was brought home that day, she was extremely sad and very discouraged.

After spending many days and hours looking forward to being somewhat "normal" like the other kids, she was told she could not stay at her neighborhood school because she had a condition that confined her to a wheel chair. The next day I paid a visit to the board of education and spoke to the director in charge of all special education programs in the school district of Montclair. The director at the central office was astonished that Felicia was denied admittance to Northeast School. The director of special education put her coat on and both of us went to speak with the principal of Northeast school. The principal was adamant about Felicia not attending classes at Northeast school but decided to concede after being admonished by the central office administrator.

Dr. O's 10 Essential Ingredients for Success   Marian Osborne, Ed D

When the director and I left the building, the director said that Felicia is welcome to attend Northeast school or any other school we choose in our neighborhood because the law said she could. After careful consideration and taking a deep breath, I made a decision. My response to that director was "I don't want my daughter in an environment that was not welcoming". The director agreed with me and Felicia was reassigned to another fifth-grade neighborhood school in Montclair New Jersey.

Although Felicia had many challenges growing up, she made a decision that she was not going to be handicapped but often let others know that she is handi-capable. Felicia continued her education and earned a bachelor's degree in Management of Information Systems and graduated with honors from New York Institute of Technology where she spent 15 years working for AT&T as a Senior Metrics & Reporting Analyst. She left that company in 2013 and began to run her own business.

She is currently the CEO of Bethel Counseling Services in Newark, New Jersey where she is able to provide leadership to a staff of 10 which consists of licensed alcohol counselors, psychiatrists, psychologist, and administrative support staff. She assisted in the policies and procedures and also developed programs for the counseling center and community. Her father and I are proud of her as she continues to meet daily challenges and reach out her hand in helping others in need. Felicia has often been referred to as the "Little Giant". She was nick named the Little Giant because of all the great things she's accomplished and being so small in stature. She was on ABC News and was interviewed on the Here and Now Show. Felicia has also been featured in her own magazine.

While my two daughters attended school each day, I continued to take classes to advance my knowledge regarding educational rights of children with disabilities. There are situations in life everyone will experience. I have learned through my experiences that having courage coupled with faith will always win in every situation.

Ingredient 5

Integrity

As a Teacher and Administrator in a Failing School District

I learned that I must and should always do the right thing even if it is difficult.

Over the years while raising my two beautiful daughters, I continued to seek to educate myself in the area of children with disabilities and school administration. As a result of having overwhelming medical bills, I researched scholarships and fellowships because I did not have the finances to pay for college tuition. I was fortunate to receive an academic scholarship at the New Jersey City University and completed my Bachelor of Arts degree in early childhood education. Although I was able to obtain a teachers' license with my bachelor's degree, I immediately applied for a Master's Fellowship program that would finance the cost of my Masters of Arts degree in urban and special education.

There were only ten individuals who received fellowships that year. There were several individuals/ professors who believed in me. I was so focused and determined that it did not go unnoticed. At Essex County College, Professor Anthony Del Tufo provided the guidance I needed at that time. Dr. Jerry Weiss took an interest in me and encouraged me to complete a master's program in education from New Jersey City University. I began my public-school teaching experience after my daughters were in junior high school. Although my teaching experience started late in life, I had spent years educating myself and was able to familiarize myself with the rights of those individuals with disabilities.

After graduating with a Master of Arts degree in Education, I accepted a job at Orange High School working with students who had behavior disabilities. They were labeled "emotional disturbed". That category now has been ruled inappropriate to label students. They are now referred to as "behavior disabled". I remember the first day of school I had more students than I had desks or chairs for. Although the New Jersey Administrative Code was very specific regarding how many students were allowed in that special classroom, my numbers exceeded the required limit. This made teaching and working with that population more challenging for me. I just borrowed chairs from other classrooms and also utilized my desk for several of my students. I refused to complain or let that situation take away from my student's learning. I became very innovative and resourceful while exhibiting a determination to succeed. The principal was very impressed with my commitment towards my students and decided to assign me to a special project.

There were several students in the school who were extremely disruptive and was sent to a program in Rahway called "Scared Straight". (Established in the 1970s, **Scared Straight programs** were used throughout the United States as a means of deterring juvenile crime. These excursions usually entailed visits by at-risk youth to adult prisons, where youth hear about the harsh reality of prison life from inmates. (*Crime Solutions.gov*) The principle assigned me to be one the teachers accompanying these students on the bus as they traveled to the designated prison. There was one particular student that even the teachers were afraid of him. He would roam the halls and go inside classrooms saying and acting as he pleased.

On our trip to Scared Straight, this student stood up on one of the seats on the bus and was screaming out of the window to other people in the community. He shouted, "hey you fagot" out of the bus window. I was sitting in front of the bus but when

Dr. O's 10 Essential Ingredients for Success   Marian Osborne, Ed D

I heard him I immediately turned around and started to reprimand him. Before I could say anything, this student said to me *"what the f--k are you looking at."* I was speechless and decided not to give him the attention he was seeking. After our visit to *"Scared Straight"* we all boarded the bus to head back to the school. On our way back to school the bus driver stopped at McDonald's restaurant for lunch. I noticed that the young man who was the most disruptive and had cursed at me going to this event was the only one who did not have any lunch. All of the other students on the bus had money to buy their lunch. I made a decision to purchase a lunch and soda and gave it to him. What a difference in his behavior on the way back to the school. I wasn't sure if it was from the experience at Rahway (scared straight) or gratitude for someone showing him kindness during lunch.

The next morning this same disruptive student was at my classroom door behaving and trying to say thank you, but the words never left his mouth. I realized that this student didn't know how to say, "thank you", but wanted me to know that he was grateful for my act of kindness. He showed up every morning at my door just to say good morning.

I always had a passion to teach even from a

little girl. After giving birth to a child with a disability who yearned to learn, my passion increased tremendously, and I was determined to aspire to be the best teacher there were. While Felicia was in elementary school, I attended Essex County College during the day. I completed two years at this junior college and graduated with honors. It was there I received student of month award and many other outstanding recognitions. Although my husband and others were impressed with my accomplishments, I was determined to learn as much as I could. I remember taking statistics with the professor who was the head of the department and felt it was the most difficult subject I had so far. I was determined to do well so I decided to spend every chance I got to study so that I could enhance my knowledge in that subject.

Upon graduation I received an academic scholarship to attend Jersey City State College which has since been named New Jersey City University. After completing my bachelor's degree in education, I was offered an opportunity to attend full time for one year to receive my master's degree. Although I was ready to go to work as a teacher, (we had just purchased our dream house) after much discussion with my husband it was decided that I should accept this offer. We sacrificed for an entire year by not having any furniture and eating beans and rice. As a result of our sacrifice, I was able to graduate again with honors and accepted a position as a special education teacher in Orange New Jersey.

Every teaching experience I had helped me become more effective in engaging students to learn. In 1992 I was offered a position with the State of New Jersey Department of Education. As County Supervisor of Child Study at the New Jersey State Department of Education, I was the only female of African descent to hold that title from 1992-1995. It was during my tenure at the State Department of Education that I coordinated all special education programs and services in Passaic County to ensure compliance with federal and state rules and regulations I participated in the implementation of state monitoring of school districts to ensure compliance in the areas of pupil performance, curriculum core course proficiencies, certification, facilities standards and mandated programs.

I can remember several incidents that occurred while I was the County Supervisor of Child Study. My supervisor was the County Superintendent who managed all the county superintendents in that county.

I was part of her team and we met with all the representatives of each school district once a month. There were about 50-75 individuals attending at each meeting. I was the only female person of color at each meeting during my tenure at the state. I remember one meeting when the health department was invited to speak to all the school superintendents regarding the status of HIV and AIDS. That day the room was packed with other invited guests which came to about 100 individuals attending this special informational meeting. As the presenter began to talk about the problems facing each community, he also spelled out that this condition was primarily focused on certain populations or groups of people. He indicated that those who engaged in homosexual activities were at risk. He then proceeded to say that African American females were more at risk because of their promiscuity.

I was the only African American female in the entire room, and I was sitting up front where everyone could see me. If there was a hole in the floor, I would have tried to escape inside it with those statements that were made by the presenter. I felt this gentleman could have been a little more sensitive in his presentation. His statements implied that all black females were promiscuous and therefore had a greater risk for HIV. During my tenure at the New Jersey State Department of Education, there was one school district in the entire county that was predominantly a minority district. The superintendent of that district was a male of African descent who rarely attended these monthly roundtable meetings with the county superintendent. As a result of his non-attendance, the county superintendent (my supervisor) did not care for this particular school superintendent. My supervisor often made negative comments about him in her office.

I believe he, also, had a dislike for her. This certain superintendent usually sent a representative from his district or no one showed up at all at these meetings in which she facilitated. My supervisor regarded his nonattendance as an act of disrespect. This non-attending superintendent was the superintendent of the third largest school district in the state of New Jersey. This school district test scores were so poor that the state of New Jersey took over that school district. (*State controlled school district*) It was the only state controlled school district in the entire county in which I supervised their special education programs.

One day the assistant superintendent of this minority school district asked if I would come and work at this state-controlled school district. He asked me several times to work as his director of special services. Knowing the failures and all of the challenges they faced, (I was the state monitor who evaluated them) I thanked him and politely said no thank you.

After being pursued by this assistant superintendent over a period of time and offering me a salary that amounted to a 30% raise above what I was currently making, I conceded and said I would come and help bring the district into compliance. I was well versed in the New Jersey Administrative Code that governs special education students and their programs. I was also one of the monitors who failed that district while working for the state. After joining this district in 1995, (state controlled) I realized immediately I had many challenges.

The district's special education programs had not passed compliance with the state during their yearly monitoring for over 10 years. This was unacceptable to me. Integrity was something I needed to exercise in order to turn this district around. I had to be uncompromising when it came to making decisions regarding the welfare of children. I knew my job would be a difficult one. The district's required student records (IEP'S) were all hand written which made it difficult to read and implement. After putting a plan together and building relationships with my staff, I started addressing all areas of non-compliance. I did have an advantage since I was the state monitor who monitored/evaluated their special education programs over several years and I was well aware of the non-compliant areas that needed attention. My faith was such a major part of my life that I was confident it was possible to turn bad into good and then into great in the most unlikely situations. By embracing faith, tenacity, and now integrity, I knew that as a team we could accomplish the goal of bringing the district into compliance regardless of all the problems that we faced. It was a district where it was difficult to get parents involved.

When families scarcely have jobs or food to sustain them, often education isn't a priority. I learned that if I provided dinner and child care for the parents, they seem to attend parent meetings more frequently. I believe the difficulties that were in my department were not just a district problem but a human problem. I also learned that programs become great because of the people that run them are great.

I knew that I needed to provide hope and encouragement to all my staff and then we could begin to see great productivity in our department while moving towards compliance. My staff and I began to see the light at the end of the tunnel. We were able to computerize the IEP's; we developed programs for our autistic population and eventually our district program became a model for the state of New Jersey. Although decisions were made based on integrity and what would benefit students, we were able to save the district thousands of dollars by bringing students back to the district from their out of district placements. We also were able to pass (met compliancy) on all the areas in the special education programs that were monitored that year in special education. We were compliant on all indicators monitored that year. (Letter of Congratulations, page 65)

After I was able to provide training for my teachers, child study team, and support staff, the New Jersey state department of education sent a letter to my superintendent (supervisor) asking him to release me to help the New Jersey State Department of Education train 116 other school districts. (Letter from the state on page 66). Our department's state reports were always on time and accurate. I learned in order to be successful, you must come early and be willing to stay late and always try to adhere to moral and ethical principles.

<mark>Dr. O's 10 Essential Ingredients for Success   Marian Osborne, Ed D</mark>

The ▮▮▮▮▮ Public Schools
33-35 Church Street
▮▮▮▮▮, New Jersey 07505
(973) 881-6207/6215
Fax (973) 279-4135

Dr. Clarence C. Hoover, III
Assistant Superintendent
for School Operations

MEMORANDUM # 99-69

MEMORANDUM

TO: Mrs. Marian Osborne, Director of Special Services

FROM: Dr. Clarence C. Hoover, III, Assistant Superintendent

RE: Special Education Compliance

DATE: September 23, 1998

Congratulations !!! For the past seven years the ▮▮▮▮▮ Public Schools have been attempting to become compliant with state regulations as it relates to the division of Special Education. As you may remember, one of the tasks and challenges put before you was to help the district achieve state certification by developing a corrective action plan for Special Education. Your comprehensive plan, coupled with your astute leadership have paid off in a big way. Congratulations on meeting all the requirements for state certification within the division of Special Education. This was no small accomplishment. Keep up the good work !!!

ah

C: Dr. ▮▮▮▮▮
     Personnel File

"All Children Can Learn"

Dr. O's 10 Essential Ingredients for Success   Marian Osborne, Ed D

State of New Jersey
DEPARTMENT OF EDUCATION
PO Box 500
TRENTON NJ 08625-0500

CHRISTINE TODD WHITMAN
Governor

DAVID C. HESPE
Commissioner

September 20, 2000

Dr. ▮▮▮▮▮ State District Superintendent
Paterson State-Operated School District
33-35 Church Street
▮▮▮▮▮ NJ 07505

Dear Dr. ▮▮▮,

Once again, I would like to take this opportunity to thank you for your district's participation in the self-assessment process and ask your assistance in preparing the 118 districts that will be participating in the self-assessment process during the 2000-2001 school year.

Two meetings will be scheduled in October to provide these districts with technical assistance regarding the self-assessment process. The Office of Special Education Programs would like to have Dr. Marion Osborne and a few members of the steering committee participate in these two sessions to review the process the ▮▮▮▮▮ State-Operated School District followed to complete the self-assessment document. The department feels that under the direction of Dr. Osborne, the steering committee was able to follow a process that resulted in a comprehensive review of the district's special education program. Her knowledge and leadership will be an asset to me and my staff during these scheduled technical assistance meetings. These two half day meetings will be conducted at the Edison PIRC on October 10th and 11th.

Thank you for your consideration.

Sincerely,

Barbara Gantwerk, Director
Office of Special Education Programs

BG/mz

c: Barbara Anderson
    Ben Rarick
    Marion Osborne

www.state.nj.us/education
New Jersey Is An Equal Opportunity Employer • Printed on Recycled and Recyclable Paper

Ingredient 6

Humility

Diagnosed with a Brain Tumor

I once heard someone say: *"True humility is not thinking less of yourself, it is thinking of yourself less"*

I love God with all of my heart. I am a Christian, I try to live a clean life, I read my bible regularly, I make an effort to eat healthy, I love other people no matter what they look like or what their social or financial status, I pay my bills and government taxes, I am a faithful wife, I am a loyal friend, I am a great citizen, and I am a generous giver. None of the above mattered. I was still diagnosed with a brain tumor in 2011. Everyone in life will experience some form of challenge but this diagnosis really humbled me. This experience seemed to rid me of any type of pride I might have had. I realized, at that point in time, how precious life was.

I was having trouble with my vision and made an appointment to see the eye doctor. Knowing that I was approaching 62 years of age, I surely thought my sight had begun to wane. The doctor completed a thorough evaluation but left out one test. She indicated to me this peripheral test takes 20 minutes and scheduled me to come back at a future date. Unfortunately, the date she gave me there was a snow storm which prevented me from keeping my appointment. I made a decision not to reschedule and waited an entire year before going back to the eye doctor. I was bumping into walls at the mall and I had difficulty seeing. My images were cloudy, and my letters were double vision. I eventually rescheduled my appointment.

My new appointment was in September and I was also scheduled to meet my husband afterwards at the BMW dealership. I was turning 62 years of age and he was purchasing a new car for me. I was excited as I traveled to the eye doctor to be tested. When the doctor completed my peripheral examination, she became very disturbed. She said, "You have a brain tumor. You must see a neurosurgeon." She proceeded to have me sign a form which indicated that she was not responsible but had done her job. After hearing from the eye doctor, the excitement of picking up a new car diminished. I felt that I was walking in a fog. I kept processing what the doctor had said over and over in my head. You have a brain tumor, you have a brain tumor.

When I got to the car dealership, there was no time to converse with Reggie regarding this devastating news. I had a solemn look on my face until Reggie asked me what was wrong. He could recognize the excitement I exhibited this morning was no longer evident by my facial expression. We went through the tedious paperwork of accessing our new car.

When we were on our way home, I communicated to Reggie what the doctor had said. I had a brain tumor and I needed to see a neuro-surgeon. Reggie seemed to be at peace as he began to quote God's word to me. "And we know that all things work together for good to them that love God. (Romans 8:38 KJV) He began to talk to me and encourage me. He said with confidence that we would get through this. "Don't worry". I began to realize that I had allowed words someone else had spoken to me to bring about sadness. I also realized and reminded myself that I was a child of faith and that victory was on my side. The weapon had been formed but would not prosper.

Every human being will go through a difficult time in their life but it's much better to know you are not facing life's issues alone. My faith in God sustained my sanity and helped me stay calm during this entire process. I have a tendency to hold things in and not share with too many others my difficulties because I don't want to burden them. I quickly realized that we do need each other. It's great to have a higher power and faith, but it's also comforting to have someone in your life that also has faith and can hold your hand during these tough times.

I remember how my mother would always read stories to us about the life challenges of different characters in the Bible. In particular, I loved the story of the three Hebrew boys. My mom would read to us about Shadrach, Meshach, and Abednego, who lived in the land of King Nebuchadnezzar. These boys loved God and dedicated their lives to worshipping only Him. They would not bow down to any other god but their God, and of course they wouldn't bow down to the golden statue of the King. Well as the story goes, there were men who knew that the Hebrew boys were not doing as the King ordered so they told King Nebuchadnezzar.

The King was very angry about this, so he sent for the boys. As they were brought before him, the King said "Is it true, that you do not worship the golden image which I have set up? If you do not, I will cast you into the burning fiery furnace." The three Hebrew boys told the King that even if he threw them into the furnace they could not bow down to the golden statue. The King was furious! He told the guards to heat up his furnace seven times hotter than usual. He then commanded the mightiest men in his army to tie the Hebrew boys up and throw them into the fiery furnace. The guards did as they were told. As the King looked into the furnace he was amazed at what he saw. There was Shadrach, Meshach and Abednego walking in the midst of the fiery furnace unhurt. Not only did the King see the three Hebrew boys but also there was a fourth person who looked like the Son of God (Daniel 3) in there with them! I believed that although I was going through this fiery furnace or this difficult time in my life, I refused to give in to negative thoughts. I believed that I would come out victorious.

As I got up the next morning, I began to map out my day and coming weeks. I knew I wanted to get a second opinion from another eye doctor. I made an appointment with another eye specialist who had me take an MRI with contrast. *(this is when they take a picture while shooting dye into your brain.) After* the examination, the technician gave me a certain look but did not speak of the results. I asked her about what she saw in the x-ray and she replied she would be sending the results to my eye doctor. She indicated that she was not allowed to share the results with me. When I returned to my eye doctor, she had a sad look on her face. She said, "Yes you have a pituitary adenoma" (Tumor on the pituitary part of the brain). This tumor was resting on my optic nerve and therefore affected my vision. She also suggested that I see a neurosurgeon and she gave me several names and numbers of neurosurgeons for me to make an appointment.

I began to research pituitary adenoma on my computer and educated myself regarding the treatments available. I learned that sometimes this condition can be treated through medication, but most treatment remedies resulted in surgery. I also learned that perhaps 10-20% of people are walking around with this type of tumor, but it has not impacted their life. I could not find out why these tumors occur, but the research indicated that sometimes it occurs from a previous head injury. At the age of 10, I was involved in a train accident that resulted into a head injury. I remember as a child I had to have 13 stiches at the hospital for that injury. I don't know if that particular accident caused this tumor later on in life, but I did know with confidence that I would get through it with the help of my faith, family and friends.

I called my friend Carol and told her of my situation. Carol was someone I could talk to over the years and she also had two relatives who were neurologists. It was near the Christmas holiday and she invited me to come over for a Christmas breakfast. She indicated that her cousin and uncle (who are both neurologists and practiced together) would also be there. Although two eye doctors had told me I needed brain surgery, I was determined that no one would be cutting open my head. I was able to have a conversation with Carol's uncle and cousin, who were "neurologists", and they scheduled an appointment for me in their office. They indicated that I needed to bring my MRI results so that they could review them.

When I visited the office for an examination, the cousin began to show me the film. As she held it up to the light she said that she believes this tumor was not malignant, but that surgery was highly recommended. I asked her how she could tell the tumor was not malignant. She showed me how the tumor was wrapped around blood vessels and not penetrating through them. She also indicated that the tumor was fairly large, and I needed to see a surgeon as soon as possible. She gave me the name of a highly recognized surgeon in the area. She said unless you travel to New York, this surgeon is known to be the best in the New

Jersey area. He was also affiliated with University Hospital in Newark New Jersey which is a trauma hospital. Nevertheless, we called this surgeon's office and were told he did not have any available dates for months.

Reggie and I realized we needed to make an appointment to see a neurosurgeon as soon as possible. We began to investigate other doctors in the area. We were told that the best doctor for what I needed was at New York University Hospital. My sister Theresa had an opportunity in the past to use this doctor and highly recommended him. She said to me that she would make the appointment for me and also, she would meet me there. We traveled from New Jersey to New York City to see Neurosurgeon Dr. Chandranath Senn.

I had spent six months looking for a doctor with whom I was comfortable. As Dr. Senn reviewed my film, he gave me a smile and began to explain my condition by using a mechanical model brain on his desk. He began to take it apart and show me the pituitary. He indicated that he believed this tumor wasn't malignant and that this was his specialty. Dr. Senn gave us a feeling of confidence that we really needed to have at this point in time. He told us that the tumor was the size of a tangerine, so he would be able to remove it by going up my nose. I asked him What would be the results if I choose not to have the surgery. He said I would eventually go blind because it was resting on my optic nerve in my eye.

With little discussion, my husband and I made the decision to schedule the surgery with Dr. Senn. He then ordered several other tests. He had the radiology department at NYU hospital to redo the MRI with contrast. He also paid a visit to the technician in radiology and instructed him how he wanted the test done on a certain angle. He was very deliberate and detailed in his instructions to the technician. I was so humbled by the care and concern emanating from this neurosurgeon.

I was scheduled to see the heart doctor to determine if my heart could withstand the surgery. I was then scheduled to see the ENT (ears, nose, & throat) doctor to determine if the passageway through my nose to my brain was feasible for the surgery. Although I was scheduled for surgery, I did not miss a beat in terms of my daily routine. I continued to speak at my church on Sundays and tried to provide encouragement to those I met each day. We shared the surgery with the congregation that Sunday morning prior to the Monday operation. We asked them to remember us in prayer. I had a certain peace and a calm that came over me as I began to prepare for this major operation. My surgery was scheduled for January 31st, 2011.

My doctor had already gone over the risks of permanent blindness, infection, or death. I knew that if this was my time to leave this earth, I was prepared and ready. My sister Barbara made a decision to fly to New Jersey from Florida to spend that time with me before and after the surgery. Barbara was scheduled to stay the entire month of February. Surgery was scheduled for a Monday morning. My husband and I decided that we should spend the night at a local New York hotel in order to arrive for surgery at 6 am the next morning.

My daughter and my sister Barbara spent that night at the hotel with me. The doctor gave me a prescription of Xanax (for my nerves) to take a week before surgery and also leading up to the surgery if needed. I had such peace; I did not need the calming medication and therefore did not take it. However, my daughter Yvette said she needed a Xanax for her nerves and took one of mine before going to bed that night before the surgery. My sister Theresa and her husband stopped by to wish me well and also to pray as a family that Sunday night in New York.

Dr. O's 10 Essential Ingredients for Success   Marian Osborne, Ed D

We were up early that morning and since I could not eat, no one else had breakfast. We entered the hospital and began the pre-examination for surgery. After the aides and technician had prepared me for surgery, I was put into a waiting room outside of the operating room. I was the first one scheduled for surgery that day. My family and I waited in the waiting room and then walked in Dr. Senn and his operating team. They all took a moment to introduce themselves to me and explained what their role would be during my surgery. There was one individual who took my hand and said she would be with me the entire time and will take care of me from the beginning to the end. After my family prayed again, they kissed me, and I was rolled into the operating room. All I remember was that it seemed like one minute had passed and I was awake.

I woke up in the recovery room and was cold and my head was hurting. I remember saying "Oh my head" over and over. The nurse asked me if I was cold and proceeded to put a warm pillow under my head. She then put another warm blanket over me until I felt better. I don't remember how long I was in recovery but was told that my surgery was 7 hours. (The doctor had said it would be around 4 hours) When the nurse rolled me out of the recovery room, I could see

Dr. Senn and my family, but my vision was blurred. Dr. Senn asked me "how many fingers do I have up?" I answered correctly several times. In between his questions, I kept saying "Oh my head". He then asked me how painful was my headache on a scale of 0 to 10 with zero being no pain and 10 meaning a lot of pain. I answered him and said. "20".

Dr. Senn instructed the nurse to give me orally some pain medication. I was then rolled into intensive care. I remember that I had tubes coming out of every opening God had given me at birth and two places in both arms. There was one opening in my arm to receive medication and another one to draw blood. I don't know the purpose of the third opening in my arm - but I definitely did not enjoy having the nurses come and go taking blood and pumping medication in me constantly. I also had a drainage coming directly from my spine into a bag that was checked periodically. I stayed thirsty and needed water frequently.

I was fortunate that my sister and husband never left my side the entire time I was hospitalized. They took turns and were there during the day and also every night. That first night after surgery the nurse brought me some Jell-O. I didn't have much of an appetite. The next morning, I was told the doctor had ordered me to have another MRI with contrast. My head was still bothering me, so I begged the doctor not to move me. I did not want to be rolled anywhere. Just leave me alone and let me heal. The doctors said they would wait another day, but that procedure had to be done.

The next day I remember how painful it was to be rolled all the way to x-ray and have that procedure done. Every bump and turn caused my head to hurt. I was throwing up periodically and my head would hurt from the pressure of throwing up. I remember on the third day (Wednesday) after surgery, my doctor summoned my family to come outside of my hospital room because he wanted to talk to them. I was so nauseous and sick that I thought I was dying. I was thinking the surgeon wanted to give them some bad news because that's how bad I felt after that surgery. I found out later from my family that the doctor was so excited about the results of the surgery. He called them outside of the room so that he could show them the MRI results pre- and post-surgery. He showed them the picture of the tumor before surgery and the picture of the empty space on the brain after the tumor was removed. The doctor stated, "I believe we got it all". I remained in intensive care for seven (7) days after the surgery.

Even though my insurance indicated I could remain in intensive care for only three days, my doctor told them not to move me no matter what the insurance people approved. Dr. Senn demonstrated that he was concerned about his patient and he was also the head of neurosurgery at NYU hospital. One morning before leaving the hospital, Dr. Senn came to see me. I put my hand on my chest and said, "thank you". This talented neurosurgeon smiled and said, "don't thank me, you prayed, and God used my hands". At that moment, I knew God had been faithful to me. Although I kept looking for God to come another way and heal me, I realized that sometimes God uses doctors and people to do His work.

I decided to send Dr. Senn and his staff a plant to his office with a thank you note. I was so grateful and humbled for the excellent care given to me during this difficult time. I left the hospital to go home after eight days. I had so much gratitude that God had given me a second chance at life. I knew from this experience that humility is an ingredient every human being must embrace to be successful. I know that success can be achieved if we learn to lower our pride and not exhibit arrogance.

Ingredient 7

Know Who You Are

Cultural Identity, Racism, and Institutional Trauma

Cultural and Identity Trauma:

We must know who we are and not allow others to define who we are. My eldest granddaughter Jasmine came home from elementary school one day and was very upset. She had the opportunity to read out loud in her class a story in her text book about a girl who was of African descent. Her classmates at that time were all European decent with the exception of one other girl in the class who was from Jamaica. As Jasmine proceeded to read out loud, she came across a sentence that described the little girl in the story - *"her skin was black as dirt"*.

There was a certain unspeakable tension in that classroom. That experience for Jasmine was the result of cultural insensitivity. The authors of that public-school text book should have been wiser and should have had a more diverse staff/group to review the contents of the book before it was published. They could have used the word *chocolate* or another word to describe the dark skin of the girl in the story. In addition, our public schools across the country also have a responsibility to review text books to ensure its appropriateness for *all* students. It's unfortunate that the insensitivity of authors of children books have led to traumatic experiences for children that could have been avoided. It's also important that parents get involved in their children's education.

Of course, being the protective grandmother that I am and also being an educator, I wanted to send a message to the school regarding the need to review their textbooks and providing cultural competency training for their staff. My daughter Yvette forbade me from doing so. She comforted Jasmine but did not want to bring added attention to her family. They had two younger children who still needed to attend the same school.

It's unfortunate that cultural and identity trauma is pervasive in many public-school districts and other institutions of learning today. It even exists in our churches, restaurants, and places of employment. I do acknowledge that America has made progress over the years in the area of diversity but there's still much work to be done. I find it unfortunate that even in many houses of God, there is insensitivity towards people of different race and cultures. I have eaten at very fine restaurants and I notice that certain races are allowed to work in the kitchen or bust tables, but they are not efficient enough to wait on tables. Cultural and Identity trauma has to do with an individual's very identity and personal characteristics.

In 1997 I was accepted into a doctoral program at Seton Hall University. It was a great experience but unfortunately, I did receive negative feedback from my mentor which could be perceived as a racist remark. There were 35 students chosen from 1200 applications that year. I was fortunate to have been one of the four minority students that were accepted into this rigorous doctoral program that year. Each student was assigned a mentor whose job was to read our dissertations and react to them. I just could not seem to satisfy my professor (mentor). Every time I submitted a partial paper, he would return it unsatisfied. I didn't think much of this at first because his job was to help me perfect the finished project and to assist me towards graduation. I lived only 15 minutes from the University and worked on a full-time job.

I was so determined to finish on time that I would get up 3:00 am each morning just to complete assignments before going to work. When I attended class, and submitted parts of my paper, my mentor would return it all marked up as unsatisfactory. I would stay up sometimes all night and return the corrected paper to him the very next morning placing it in his mail box before going to work. When I was running late my devoted husband would deliver it to Seton Hall before he went to his job. Each time he marked my paper incorrect, I continued to give my corrected work back to my professor the next day. I provided him with all the corrections he had suggested. My professor always received the corrected paper from me the next day. One day my professor/mentor sent me an email and asked me a question. He said, "Why are you working so hard on this paper? Don't you know that statistics show that only 50% of the students in this class will graduate on time?"

At first, I was shocked because I thought my mentor would be happy that I demonstrated such diligence in my responding to his suggestions. After careful thought I decided to respond to his email. I said "Dr. …you are absolutely right - but I plan to be part of the 50% that graduates on time." There were many times I felt like crying because of the mistreatment I received from him. He was someone I was assigned to and who continuously made negative comments regarding my assignments. At one time he said my paper was frivolous. I always seem to muster up that resilience to bounce back because of the spiritual connection I had. I had a confidence and knew who I was. I knew I needed to speak positive words of faith and I knew I was destined for great things.

No matter how inadequate or unqualified my professor/mentor tried to make me feel, I was able to gain strength from the positive words I quoted each day. Anyone can be positive when things are going well. I realize that the way I respond to life when adversity comes will either make or break me. I made a choice to speak positive words, especially when going through a storm. Although my professor felt I wasn't smart enough to graduate on time, I was determined to graduate on time because I knew where my help came from.

My youngest granddaughter Sydney had an experience in school regarding her race. She attended a predominantly white junior high school in her neighborhood. During lunch - a white male student called her a *nigger* in front of her friends and other students during lunch break. This was embarrassing for her and very demeaning. She came home upset and shared the experience with her parents. Sydney and her siblings have been raised to be kind and respect others. Sydney's parents did report the incident and the young man was suspended from school. The school also offered counseling for my granddaughter. I strongly believe that parents need to have conversations with their children regarding respect of other cultures and races. Children need to have experiences that build character that will last a life time. Frederick Douglas said, *"It's better to build a boy than to repair a man"*.

Boys and girls grow up to be men and women. What they are taught growing up becomes a part of their everyday life. If children have not learned certain principles early in life, they are not adequately prepared for life. It's unfortunate that my inherent characteristics, race, and ethnicity have been a continuous target of ongoing discrimination, mistreatment, and denial of services. There have been times my sister and I would go shopping in upscale department stores. As soon as we begin to admire a particular item, we both noticed that someone from the store begins to follow us around the store as if we were going to steal something. These occurrences happen too often until I've decided to just to ignore them or if they are over bearing, I will let them know I'm aware that I'm being followed all around the store.

Dr. O's 10 Essential Ingredients for Success   Marian Osborne, Ed D

I believe my sister took a different approach. She will immediately stop and turn around and look the individual in the eye. I think sometimes from the repeated actions of being profiled, that my sister began to be paranoid. Every time we entered a store of this kind, my sister would anticipate someone following us around as if we were criminals. My most challenging experience happened in high school.

My adolescent years in high school were quit challenging, but it was those high school years that really inspired me to be the best that I could be today. It is unfortunate that negative experiences of racism towards children of color lasts for generations. Most of the events that have occurred in my life personally seem to have been very deliberate. During my early years I did not really recognize people's behavior as unfair treatment towards me (as a result of my inherent characteristics) until I entered high school. I just wasn't that aware of how other people saw me. My life before high school was so exciting and fulfilling. I had two parents who I knew loved me and my siblings. They demonstrated their love for us daily. I enjoyed spending time with my sisters and my brother. We lived in a house where we were able to play in a large backyard and attend the neighborhood pool. Our Christmases were awesome. Our parents were well-equipped to provide a good life for their children. We were the best well fed and well-dressed kids in our Brooklyn neighborhood.

Every Friday our father took us out to a hamburger place on Broadway. I remember my siblings ordering a hot dog, but I had to have a hamburger. I also remember the delicious frosted root beer soda we had during those family times. We looked forward to our father taking us there every Friday after work. I can also remember eating at a Chinese restaurant some evenings when my parents had to work late. Since my mom worked as a licensed beautician in Harlem, my father was responsible for us on Saturdays. My mother took us on trips to New York from Brooklyn. I remember her taking us to Coney Island on the D train. She made sure we went to the Barnum and Bailey Circus every time they came to town.

My dad would cook for us and he gave us money to go to the neighborhood movie theatre every Saturday. It wasn't until I reached 9th grade that I began to feel a difference in how I was treated, outside of our home, as a result of my personal characteristics. These occurrences became more apparent as I began my journey through life. I am so grateful that I learned lessons early in my adolescent years that the cultural and institutional trauma I was experiencing was only subjective.

My parents taught me and my siblings that it's more important how we see ourselves and not to define ourselves by how others might see us. I was determined that I would not let these experiences cause me to become bitter. In life we do have choices. Most of the time you can't control the events that occur, but you can control your responses to those events. I had a choice that I could either react negatively to these events or I could reject those trauma driven feelings and realize that situations happen to people in life all the time. I realized that I was beautifully made by God and destined to do great things. Our parents continued to drill into us that we could be anything we desired to be. They affirmed us constantly and told us how beautiful we were.

It is because of these teachings that I learned at a young age to talk to myself (spirituality) by quoting positive words of faith that I was taught in Sunday school and church. These words lifted my spirit. Believing in these Biblical phrases sustained me through many difficult situations in my life. From my childhood to this very day I understand that I am not defined by people. God does not make junk. It's so important that we know who we are.

Most therapists realize that trauma impacts an individual depending on the person's experiences, genetic makeup, individual temperament, resilience, and the degree of support available to them. I knew I had resilience and I had much support through my faith in a higher power and the love of family and friends. As I stated earlier, having healthy relationships and keeping positive thoughts helped me interrupt that cycle of trauma in my life. These relationships through my church experiences help foster a sense of belonging and community. I believe when people experience trauma, they must find a way to talk about it or it can lead to anxiety, depression, low self-esteem, or other issues that can make you want to isolate.

During my studies I've read too many times that even people taking drugs are three times more likely to have had experienced some type trauma than non-drug users. They want the pain to go away and disappear. Unfortunately, as an adolescent I wanted to hide from my pain and I wanted it to just go away. It was during my first year of high school that I was placed in an all-white special honor's math class at John Jay High School in Brooklyn, New York.

Institutional Trauma

As a result of Brown vs Board of Education in 1954, it was mandated that I attend a school in an all-white community. One of the most historical court cases, especially in terms of education 347 U.S. 483 (1954). This case took on segregation within school systems or the separation of white and black students within public schools. Up until this case, many states had laws establishing separate schools for white students and another for black students. This landmark case made those laws unconstitutional.

The decision was handed down on May 17, 1954. It overturned the *Plessy v. Ferguson* decision of 1896, which had allowed states to legalize segregation within schools. The chief justice in the case was Justice Earl Warren. His court's decision was a unanimous 9-0 decision that said, "separate educational facilities are inherently unequal." The ruling essentially led the way for the civil rights movement and essentially integration across the United States. I was mandated to attend a school that was not located in my neighborhood that I was familiar with. If racism was so prevalent during the 60's and before, something should have been done to protect those children who were mandated to attend schools outside of their neighborhoods.

I realize that individuals lost their lives so that I could have an opportunity to attend schools I choose to go to. I am grateful for the sacrifices that were made to enable me to achieve academically in various arenas. However, I do question the fact that children are still being placed in situations where they are not wanted, and this can cause irreversible and long-term damage.

In the fall of 1951, approximately 20 parents attempted to enroll their children in the closest school to their homes, but each was denied enrollment and told that they must enroll in the segregated school. This prompted a class action suit to be filed. At the district level, the court ruled in favor of the Topeka Board of Education saying that both schools were equal in regard to transportation, buildings, curriculum, and highly qualified teachers. The case then went on to the Supreme Court and was combined with four other similar suits from across the country.

This decision entitled students to receive a quality education regardless of their racial status. It also allowed for African American teachers to teach in any public school they chose, a privilege that was not granted before the Supreme Court ruling in 1954. The ruling set the foundation for the civil rights movement and gave African Americans hope that "separate, but equal" on all fronts would be changed. Unfortunately, however, desegregation was not that easy and is a project that has not been finished, even today.

As stated in an earlier chapter, my high school years were tumultuous as a result of institutional trauma. As I continued to read stories of other people of African descent who experienced cultural and institutional trauma, I gained a better understanding. I realized that I can't put too much significance into how people view me as a result of their own personal hang ups. I was able to succeed in life because of my resilience, my faith in God, and knowing who I am. I am a child of God and He wants good things for His children. God promised me through His word that *"Beloved, I wish above all things that thou may prosper and be in health, even as thy soul prospers." (3 John 1:2 NKJ)* I learned that even famous individuals were mistreated regardless of their personal successes. The one story that resonated with me was the story of Arthur Ashe.

Arthur Robert Ashe Jr. (July 10, 1943 – February 6, 1993) was an American professional tennis player. He won three Grand Slam titles. Ashe was the first black player selected to the United States Davis Cup team and the only black man ever to win the singles title at Wimbledon, the US Open, and the Australian Open. He retired in 1980. He was ranked World No. 1 by Harry Hopman in 1968 and by Lance Tingay of The Daily Telegraph and World Tennis Magazine in 1975. In the ATP computer rankings, he peaked at No. 2 in May 1976. In the early 1980s, Ashe is believed to have contracted HIV from a blood transfusion he received during heart bypass surgery.

In his book (chapter five) "Days of Grace", Arthur Ashe talks about the burden he carried regarding race. As he was being interviewed by a reporter for People magazine he knew that his life would soon come to an end. He expressed to her (the interviewer), his greatest burden he shared in life was not dying, even though he knew he had contracted a fatal condition.

The reporter said, "Mr. Ashe, I guess this must be the heaviest burden you have ever had to bear, isn't it?" she asked finally. Arthur thought for a moment, but only a moment. "No, it isn't. It's a burden, all right. But AIDS isn't the heaviest burden I have had to bear." The reporter asked "Is there something worse? Your heart attack maybe?" I didn't want to detain her, but I let the door close with both of us still inside. "You're not going to believe this, "I said to her, "but being black is the greatest burden I've had to bear." "You can't mean that." "No question about it. Race has always been my biggest burden. Having to live as a minority in America. Even now it continues to feel like an extra weight tied around me." I can still recall the surprise and perhaps even the hurt on her face. I may even have surprised myself, because I simply had never thought of comparing the two conditions before. However, I stand by my remark. Race is for me a more onerous burden than AIDS. My disease is the result of biological factors over which we, thus far, have had no control. Racism, however, is entirely made by people, and therefore it hurts and inconveniences infinitely more.

I am an optimist, not a pessimist. Still, a pall of sadness hangs over my life and the lives of almost all African Americans because of what we as a people have experienced historically in America, and what we as individuals experience each and every day. Whether one is a welfare recipient trapped in some blighted "housing project" in the inner city or a former Wimbledon champion who is easily recognized on the streets and whose home is a luxurious apartment in one of the wealthiest districts of Manhattan, the sadness is still there." *

I can relate to the pain Arthur Ashe was referring to. Having worked for the New Jersey state government and other secular positions, my experiences with racism has continued throughout my entire life. It's something I have to deal with each and every day.

*Arthur Ashe and Arnold Rampersad, _Days of Grace,_ * Alfred A Knopf, New York 1993, USA

When I go to the store, when go for a job interview, and every time I tried to pursue higher education, it (racism) has always been something I've encountered. It is my hope and prayer that all families will begin to understand the damage that is done when these attitudes are allowed to fester and grow.

It is incumbent upon each parent, teacher, employer, clergy, athlete, community leader, and any influential individual to use every opportunity they have to educate others so that we can stem these pervasive attitudes that seem to permeate throughout our communities and the world.

Taking a Knee

My husband Reginald Osborne decided to write a response article regarding the sports players taking a knee to protest systemic injustice that continues to permeate throughout the United States. Reginald was disturbed by a newspaper's article he read regarding NFL Commissioner Roger Goodell sending a letter to all 32 teams saying that he wants all players to stand for the national anthem. After sending the article to the editor of the Palm Beach Post, they decided to print his article. It stated, *"Please make note that Francis Scott Key was a slave owner who didn't see blacks as humans, but as* property. Blacks have fought and bled in every war that our nation has been involved in. Blacks fought and died in the Civil War, Revolutionary War, the Spanish American War, World War I, World War II, Korean War, Vietnam War, etc. Blacks did not come to America on the Mayflower but in slave ships. When our ancestors came here, thousands were hung from trees and thousands were murdered by the Ku Klux Klan and other hate groups. My family members have fought in wars and "conflicts". This includes my father and two brothers who became disabled in WWII and the Vietnam War. Injustice continues to take place against people of color, especially by the few police who have murdered blacks, and all have been found to be innocent. I have one question: "If Hitler had written the national anthem, would all 32 teams and all Americans stand?" I think not.

Most blacks, when they don't see diversity in our political leaders, say that "we don't feel a part" says The Palm Beach Post - Sunday, October 15, 2017 in an article entitled *Injustice Wears on for Blacks*.

Misty Copeland:

A True Role Model for Girls of Color

I read an article about a talented Black dancer with the renowned American Ballet Theatre. She was featured in the Palm Beach Post on Sunday, August 16, 2015.

Dr. O's 10 Essential Ingredients for Success   Marian Osborne, Ed D

The article was entitled *"Copeland, role model black girls have needed."* The accomplishments of this dancer are so important for young girls of color and also girls of all races. It's important for children to grow up with role models and individuals they can look up to help validate them. Children not being able to be validated can have a negative impact on them physically, mentally, and emotionally. Not to be able to see a reflection of themselves leads to feelings of exclusion and isolation. Misty Copeland is an example of when you are confident in whom you are, you're destined to achieve greater things in life.

Misty describes her life growing up as being the only black girl in her dance classes and reading magazines and attending shows never featuring black women who looked like her. The article summed it up by stating: *"If you want to make a human being into a monster, deny them, at the cultural level, any reflection of themselves."* What I related to was the fact that Misty didn't allow people or society to define her. She was confident in knowing she was beautifully made by God and she could aspire to be great in spite of not seeing reflections of herself.

Ingredient 8

Be Loving

A Gift from God – "My Wife"
Written by Reginald C Osborne Jr.

When you exhibit love towards everyone you meet, kind people are drawn into your life like a magnet. It's very difficult not to be successful in life when you are surrounded by individuals who are positive about making a difference in other people's lives.

Mother Teresa said:

"Love-The One Creative Force"

Spread love everywhere you go: first of all, in your own house. Give love to your children, to your wife or husband, to a next-door neighbor.... Let no one ever come to you without leaving better and happier. Be the living expression of God's kindness; kindness in your face, kindness in your eyes, kindness in your smile, kindness in your warm greeting.

On September 30, 1967 I waited patiently at our church altar in Brooklyn New York with my two best men. They were my eldest brother Bobby and my now brother in- law Rufus. As we waited at the altar, tears of joy ran down my face. I thought about how I met my soon to be bride. It began in June 1965.

When I was in high school, I use to sing in a group called Joyce and the four friends. We sang all over the metropolitan area of New Jersey and New York. We sang in night clubs, bars, talent shows on street corners etc. Joyce was our lead singer along with Dorian, David, Adolphus and me. As I waited at the church altar I remembered how we use to drink a bottle of wine and smoke weed before each performance.

One Friday evening in June 1965, our group was on the corner singing some rock and roll songs. The harmony was fantastic. I always carried a bottle of tiger rose wine in my back pocket. As we were singing, we began to talk about a church in Newark located at 505 Central Avenue. It was called The Newark Deliverance Evangelistic Center which had a 500-voice choir. Most of the choir members were good-looking females. After drinking some more wine and smoking more weed our singing group decided to go to this church to check these church girls out.

We arrived at the church at around 7:30 pm and were greeted by two ushers who sat us in the balcony. (the building use to be a movie theatre) A few minutes later the choir came out singing and marching. The four of us were amazed because there were so many young people male and female. We were excited that there were more females than males in this choir. That evening I spotted my gift from God - who was one of the females singing and marching with that choir. As I sat with my eyes focused on her, the pastor (whose name was Arturo Skinner) came to the stage and began speaking. He spoke about God's love for people. After he finished his message, he looked up in the balcony and said, "I would like to pray for that young feller in the balcony". He was looking at and speaking directly to me. I eventually got up out of my seat and went to the front of the church as the pastor requested.

My friends were laughing at me because as Pastor Skinner prayed for me, I fell to the floor and the wine bottle broke in my back pocket. (It was a miracle that I didn't get cut by the glass from the wine bottle) When I returned to my seat my friends were laughing so hard that the ushers requested that they leave the building until they could refrain from laughing and calm down. Although my friends and I decided to leave the church at the end of that evening, I knew that I had to return that coming Sunday. I knew that what I had experienced that evening after the pastor prayed for me felt better than wine and weed put together.

Dr. O's 10 Essential Ingredients for Success   Marian Osborne, Ed D

In addition, I wanted to see and meet that beautiful young lady with those sexy legs once again. It had been almost eight years when I had first felt that liberating feeling in church. I remember attending church at the age of thirteen. A Pastor whose name was Bill Iverson prayed for me, but I just didn't stay connected to the church. However, at the age of twenty-one, Pastor Arturo Skinner prayed for me that June evening and I knew then it was time for me to stay connected to the church. I made a decision then to become active in that church although my mind and heart was always on how I could get to know Marian Crew. Many times, I would speak to Pastor Skinner about my overwhelming feelings for Marian. He would encourage me to   continue to pray and seek God first.

One day Pastor Skinner selected Marian and I to head up a youth program and this is how we became acquainted with each other. When we were together preparing for this youth program, I use to look at her and say to myself how beautiful and sexy she was. I wanted to kiss her all over and tell her how much I loved her and needed her in my life. She did most of the planning for this youth program, because my mind was constantly on her. I don't think she was aware of my adoration for her. My wife is today more beautiful and sexy than she was 53 years ago when I first met her.

Dr. O's 10 Essential Ingredients for Success   Marian Osborne, Ed D

I became aware that there were three other young men in church who spoke to me about Marian. They said that they also had an interest in her. We all shook hands and said, "May the best man win". Well, you know who won. I guess the best man won because we got married on September 30, 1967 at the Brooklyn Deliverance Evangelistic Center in Brooklyn, New York. God has blessed us with two beautiful daughters - the eldest is Felicia and the youngest is Yvette. They both have the same spirit and beauty as their mother. Marian has been such a blessing and encouragement to me for over fifty years in which we have been married. I am now an associate pastor and she is a doctor in education. Our two daughters along with our three grandchildren have been so blessed. Our eldest daughter has her own company and the youngest is a computer science engineer. Our youngest daughter's husband Earl is a principle at an elementary school in New Jersey. We are so proud of our entire family.

I worked for many years as a research and development technician at Domino Sugar Company in Brooklyn New York. Marian worked alongside of me while attending school to become a special education teacher. We worked together and made many sacrifices in order to support our daughters. When the girls were in elementary school we decided to move to Montclair, New Jersey which we believed would provide our daughters with an excellent educational experience. We saved our money and purchased a six-family house in Montclair. We bought this house as is, which meant we had to do a lot of work on that house such as painting, plumbing and electrical. As we worked together on that old house we were blessed to have four tenants who we allowed to pay a very low rent because they were senior citizens with minimal means of support. These tenants were consistent rent payers, but they only had their monthly social security checks. We knew by being kind and loving, it would come back to us.

    I believe that God helped us during those tough times because we were sensitive and kind to those who needed help. We occupied two of the four apartments for our immediate family. This was a very difficult period time in our life as I had to commute to my job in Brooklyn, New York from our home in Montclair New Jersey. Our daughter Felicia was born with a bone illness called osteogenesis imperfecta which means she had soft bones. The two hospitals in Montclair along with Felicia's orthopedic doctor knew us by name because they saw us as we bought Felicia to them many times. We are so grateful for the help that they provided for us. The medical bills were overwhelming and such a burdened to us, but Marian and I worked and stayed together to provide for our family.

I remember paying two dollars each month to the hospitals and Felicia's doctor. Our church and biological family were so supportive to us during those difficult times. We remember how Marian's sister Barbara bought Felicia a coat when Felicia was in the hospital with a broken femur. Felicia had spent months in the hospital and it was a cold winter day and we didn't have money to buy our daughter a coat to bring her home. We have a lot of gratitude for family and friends who have been there for us during tough times.

Marian continued to attend New Jersey City University to obtain her master's degree in education and to become a special education teacher. Due to her constantly making the dean's list we didn't have to pay for her education. I continued to work at Domino Sugar Company and once again we had more money to save. We sold our six-unit house and bought our first single family home on Willowmere Avenue in Montclair New Jersey where we spent 33 years. My work continued at Domino Sugar and Marian worked at Orange High School in Orange, New Jersey. At this time Marian stated that she would like to obtain a doctorate degree at Seton Hall University.

Out of hundreds of other applicants who applied to be accepted in this extremely rigorous doctoral program, my wife was accepted and in May of 1999, she became Marian Osborne Ed. D., with honors. We both had a passion to help other people but wasn't sure how or where we could help. It was during this time in our life we both began to volunteer our time at a residential drug program in Verona, New Jersey. This program was a 28-day inpatient alcohol and substance abuse program. That is where my wife and I realized that we wanted to devote our lives to working with alcoholics and drug addicts. Once again, my wife, whom I call a gift from God, returned to school and became a license certified alcohol and drug counselor while she was still a school administrator. She began to look at a second career when she retired.

When we moved to Florida, Marian also became a master's level certified addiction professional (MCAP) after taking a state test. She has recently met the requirements for and recently received her certified mental health professional certificate from Florida's certification (CMHP) board. We both are licensed in the addiction field and have met the requirements for certified relapse prevention specialist.

In addition, my wife took a very difficult course with Dr. Terrance Gorsky and has become an advanced certified relapse prevention specialist (ACRPS). I am not bragging about my wife, but she has been such a blessing to so many and has encouraged so many to return to school. Education is one of the keys to be a success in life.

In 2001 we bought a building in Newark New Jersey on Pierce Street which use to be a bar. The bar was named the Dick and Ann's bar. This building eventually became an outpatient alcohol and drug treatment program in 2009. We were able to hire a psychiatrist and licensed substance abuse counselors (LCADC) to serve those sick and suffering from the disease of addiction. We received referrals from welfare, Essex County drug court, probation, and also from parole and family court. We were very busy six days a week because of the number of individuals suffering with this disease of addiction. We learned from our experiences working with clients that everyone is important and valued no matter from what walk of life they entered our program. We had lawyers, doctors, welfare recipients, gang members, and individuals from different religions. Everyone was welcome. We also made a decision to utilize the building on Sundays for spiritual support for those with the disease of addiction.

Although we were Christians we didn't condemn any person's religious belief, but we taught the importance of loving the God of your own understanding and the value of simply loving people. One of my favorite sermons is found in the Bible in *1 John 4: 20, 21(NIV)* where it states; *"Whoever claims to love God yet hates a brother (or sister) is a liar. For whoever does not love their brother and sister, whom they have seen, cannot love God whom they have not seen."*

In November of 2013 after breaking my leg, Marian and I decided to move to our vacation home in Delray Beach Florida. We have been extremely happy since coming to the sunshine State. Delray Beach, Florida is noted for having the greatest amount of drug rehabilitation programs in the nation for those who have substance abuse problems. Once again, I give God the credit for blessing me with my precious gift- my wife Dr. Marian Osborne. She is the love of my life and has exhibited such a loving spirit.

Reggie & Marian

Dr. O's 10 Essential Ingredients for Success   Marian Osborne, Ed D

Reggie & Marian Holiday Vacations

Celebrating
50 Years of Marriage

Ingredient 9

Be Laser Focused

What Can Be Done to Improve the Quality of Life

There are definite changes that need to take place in our country and communities that could reduce the negative consequences of traumatic experiences for children, adolescents, and adults experiencing *cultural* and *institutional* trauma. Too often many of these experiences that individuals are confronted with in life can be avoided if major changes were to take place in our country and society as a whole.

Some traumas are caused by *sicknesses, death of a loved one, job loss, addictions, poverty, unfair incarcerations, victims of violence, homelessness, inadequate health care, racism,* and more. Although some traumas are unavoidable, I have come to understand as a therapist that the more an individual is fortified with spirituality, (not religion) they have the ability to rise above their circumstances, and stay connected to positive people, places, and things the greater their chances are of surviving these traumatic experiences. I have personally experienced that individuals do get back up after a fall. It is unfortunate that many individuals experiencing trauma become anxious, depressed, and unable to function effectively in life as a result of their traumatic experiences.

As I was receiving my training as a therapist, one of my professors said these words of wisdom to the class. He said, *"if you have experienced trauma in your life, you must find a way to talk about it, you must tell your story."* I have learned personally that talking about or sharing your pain can be liberating. I realize that individuals who hold traumatic experiences inside and do not have a medium to vent, they are not able to live a fulfilled life. It's important for me to tell my story so that I will continue to heal as I journey on throughout my life. It's also healing for me as I learn to desensitize myself and not allow outside forces to interrupt my peace, safety or wellbeing.

Although many individuals have found ways to avoid the consequences of some traumas, there needs to be another review of what was suggested by the Kerner Report of 1968.

Some Suggested Ways to Minimize the Consequences of Some Traumas Experienced by Individuals

The Kerner Report of 1968

In July 28, 1967 President Johnson established a Commission and directed them to answer three basic questions regarding civil disorders that were taking place throughout the United States. It needs to be understood that individuals experiencing certain traumas often have a tendency to behave in ways that may not be acceptable to society at large as a result of their frustrations. There were so many disturbances throughout the United States in the inner-cities during the 60's that president Johnson felt something needed to be done. The president wanted to know what happened. Why did it happen, and what can be done to prevent it from happening again? *

It is enormously important for me as I review this report relate it to today. (2018) Looking back over 50 years I realize that not much has changed today. The same conditions within those cities which encouraged riots and disturbances across our country during 1967 still exist today. Unfortunately, our current government officials have not demonstrated a concern for those conditions outlined in the report of 1968. As a matter of fact, the conditions in those cities have been magnified with our current suggested governmental policies emanating from the white house. The Kerner Commission was careful, and laser focused in assessing the causes of these individual rebellions, and was able to identify conditions that were prevalent, and which led to the causes of so much violence which took place in those cities during the 1960's.

According to the report, disruptions didn't come as a result of one incident, but the disorder was generated from an increasingly disturbed social atmosphere. Unfortunately, there were months of incidents that contributed to the unrest which existed within those communities. There were continuous issues that were ignored or never addressed. It seems that it was a bank of continuous grievances that led to the violence that occurred in those cities of people of color. Often it is one incident that ignites the fire that spills over into the behaviors that link to violence. Although there is no justification for violence, when a group of people have been denied their human rights for so many years, they become hopeless and at times reach a point where they no longer value their lives or the lives of others.

The Kerner report suggested that there were several incidents that caused increased tension during that time which led to the violence. Most of those incidents surveyed by the commission were police actions. It was also noted in the Kerner report that the police actions in almost half of the cases were incidents which led to the outbreak of civil disorder. Twelve out of the twenty-four incidents of disorder were the direct results of police final actions.

Those involved in the civil disorder expressed a need to have full participation in society and have material benefits that are enjoyed by most American citizens. The Commission's report considered the nature of the complaints. It was also noted that there was an urgency in meeting the demands that were outlined in the report.

I have worked in some of these communities and can validate the existence of these conditions. I can recall almost every relative of mine have been inappropriately stopped by the police at least two times and that includes my husband and me.

One evening my husband and I were out visiting some friends in East Orange New Jersey. We have never been arrested, never had any lingering tickets, always carried car insurance, and made sure our license plate was up to date. Our car was stopped, and we were surrounded by at least four police cars. One officer got out the car and with a bullhorn ordered us to get out of our car. I was surprised but I also noticed a

Dr. O's 10 Essential Ingredients for Success   Marian Osborne, Ed D

fear that swept over my husband's face. He turned and said to me; "do not say anything and I will do the talking". Looking back in retrospect I had no understanding as to what he meant "don't say anything".

The officer with the bullhorn instructed both of us to move away from our car and they wanted to see my husband's driver's license. Then they proceeded to ask for the insurance card. I was so perplexed because I did not know why we were being stopped or being treated as criminals. Although my husband asked me not to say anything, I just had to say something. "Why are we being stopped?" I asked the officer. He looked at me but did not respond. My husband was so nervous that he began to drop his papers that were in his wallet while locating his license.

I started to become annoyed and asked the question again. "Why are we being stopped" I need to say that all of these officers were of European decent and none looked like me. They had us standing for a long time in the freezing cold outside of the warmth of our car. My annoyance turned into anger and I began to say other things to the police even though I knew my husband had instructed me not to speak.

Those who know me know that I am not one for not saying something when I feel I am being unfairly treated. After they had taken and reviewed my husband's license, they then asked my husband could they search his car. Before my husband could speak, I answered and said, "do you have a search warrant?" My husband gave me that disapproving look and said to the officer "Oh yes officer, you can search the car".

After my husband's penetrating gaze, I felt I needed to be quiet. After the officers searched our car, they indicated we could go. I was so furious I said to them again "why were we stopped?" The officer then looked at me and said, "we received a report about a car with your description in the neighborhood." My husband smiled at the officer and said have a good night. I knew I was going to get it when we left the scene. My husband said, *didn't I tell you not to say anything."?* I responded "why" He said when it comes to black men; cops are known to shot first and ask questions later. That was my first lesson of how one should behave when you're black and you are stopped by the police.

The Kerner report also explained the seriousness of the gap between black and white citizens with respect to important elements of life quality. It was evident that the people living in these cities were underserved socially and economically when compared to white families. People of color had completed fewer years of education and fewer had attended high school. People of color were twice as likely to be unemployed and three times as likely to be in unskilled in-service jobs. People of color averaged 70 percent of the income earned by whites and were more than twice as likely to be living in poverty.

In addition, the Kerner report suggested that there were racial gaps, there were health disparities, infant mortality was higher, greater disease incidences, and those living in those communities of color did not live as long as their white counterparts. Unfortunately, people who have years of frustration built up will lash out when they come to that breaking point of powerlessness. I have witnessed this first hand working as a service provider in Newark New Jersey for twelve years. I have also witnessed this as a teacher and school administrator working in an underserved community.

Education in our democratic society should equip all children so that they can develop their potential and participate fully in our American life. School failure can be traumatizing for many students. When our schools have failed to provide the educational experience, which could overcome the effects of discrimination and deprivation for our children we become a nation that fosters discontent. Failure to provide effective education within communities of color across our nation has been one of the greatest misfortunes which have led to crimes and the deterioration of our cities in America.

According to the Kerner report the most dramatic evidence of the relationship between educational practices and civil disorders lies in the high incidences of riot participation by minority youth who have not completed high school. Unfortunately, 50 years haven't brought us much change.

In 2018 our young people are still unemployed; our public schools are still producing students who don't have what they need to succeed in life, and the excessive use of deadly force by police are still being perpetrated against our young men of color. The progress which has been made since slavery will have accomplished nothing if the problem of students failing isn't dealt with.

We do not have to continue to study these communities of color for the answers. It's unfortunate that our public schools have selected a range of mental problems and skills which are so narrow that the schools have failed to develop much of the potential of children of color. It's definitely a time for a reassessment of our public-school policies. It's time for us to be laser focused if our children are going to experience success in school and in life. "If monkeys can be taught sign language, and if one monkey can instruct another one in sign, and if a gorilla can acquire a 90 on a human IQ test, then one would think that children of color could be taught by their teachers and succeed in school."** Everyone needs to re-read the Kerner Commission Report; and we need to act on its wise recommendations.

*Kerner Report of the National Advisory Commission on Civil Disorders (New York: Bantam Books, 1968) pp.1-29

**Asa G. Hilliard, *Language, Culture, and Assessment.* U.S. Educational Resources Information Center ERIC Document ED 191973, 1980

Elie Wiesel is a holocaust survivor and writer who stated: *"I swore never to be silent whenever and wherever human beings endure suffering and humiliation. We must take sides. Neutrality helps the oppressor, never the victim. Silence encourages the tormenter, never the tormented."*

How Can We Make a Difference in the Lives of Others Who Have Been Underserved?

The only way to make a difference in the lives of others is to live your life as a giver and be open to love every human being God created. Being laser focused for me is making sure I assist others along the way. While I'm striving to be successful, I need to be conscious of other people's desire to be successful. Some people don't understand this statement. I strongly believe that no matter how you were raised or how you were taught to believe, we must all see ourselves as our brother's (sister) keeper. Life is short and it's important that people begin to understand that we need each other.

I love the story my husband tells often when he is speaking to an audience. He talks about a five-year-old little boy who wanted his father to play with him. His father was tired after work and just wanted to watch the football game undisturbed. The father took a magazine and found a picture of a world and ripped it up in many pieces. He then gave it to his five-year-old and told him to go into the next room and put the picture of the world back together again. The father believed this would take some time and he could watch the game. Within five minutes the little boy returned and had put the picture of the world back together. The father thought perhaps he had a genus of a son, but he did ask his son how he completed this task so fast. His son looked at his father with a smile on his face and said "It was easy daddy, on the other side of the picture of the world was a picture of a man. When I got the man right then the world got right" We all must examine ourselves and make sure that we are doing our part.

Although we are faced with many challenges in this world, each one of us can make a difference by being laser focused. We must be deliberate and intentional in accepting people of different background, faiths and cultures. We must not prejudge but judge people based on how they treat others. If we want to be effective in the lives of others, we must have the ability to stand in someone else's shoes. We must imagine experiencing what they experience and try to understand how it has impacted their lives.

I believe in life that we become successful by lifting others up. Being laser focused also will be beneficial to us as we see the need to change as we grow in knowledge.

Neuroplasticity (God and the Brain)

What is neuroplasticity? Neuroplasticity is the ability of the human brain to structurally rearrange itself in response to a wide variety of positive and negative events.* I have always enjoyed reading books regarding studies that have been done on the brain. I was the kid growing up who always asked questions like: "why is the sky blue?" or "where do babies come from?"

The brain is something, that as an adult, I have been fascinated with learning more about. According to Dr. Andrew Newberg and Mark Robert Waldman God will change your brain, but he also points out that meditating on negativity can also change your brain.**

Because we carry neuro-brain cells in everything we do, there is a need to form new beliefs and perceptions. We can change the way we think about people and our situations through practice if we are laser focused. This takes continual practice over and over again uttering positive words and phrases.

N*europlasticity* (re-wiring of the brain) sometimes we must begin to validate ourselves especially when others do not. We need to look in the mirror and say to that person "you are beautifully made by God."

I'm grateful that I have changed my way of thinking. Changing my way of thinking has been a process for me. Working with school personnel early in my teaching career – my thinking was so different 30 years ago. I used to sit in the teacher's cafeteria each day as I listen to other teachers complaining about students not learning and how these students were so misbehaved. The teachers often referenced these students regarding their parent's inability to control their own children and then expected the school to work miracles. There was always talk about how impoverished those students were and how they came from broken homes where there were no emphases on education. As a new teacher at that time, I was slightly influenced by those more veteran teachers. None the less as I began to work with my students, I realized what a wonderful group of students I've been blessed with to teach.

*Sharon Begley's book, *Train Your Mind, Change Your Brain* (Ballantine, 2007) provides one of the best and easiest reads of neuroplasticity and the brain's potential to be changed through meditation.

**Andrew Newberg, M.D., and Mark Robert Waldman, *How God Changes Your Brain* (2009) – Breakthrough findings from a leading neuroscientist.

Dr. O's 10 Essential Ingredients for Success   Marian Osborne, Ed D

Over the years, I came to know them and their struggling families. Their parents worked hard from week to week just to earn enough money to keep food on the table and shelter over their heads. I have learned that being poor doesn't make you a bad person. Children don't choose their circumstances growing up. Although I have never experienced poverty, it's my responsibility to be a blessing to those who are less fortunate than me. Unfortunately, we don't pick our family or how we are reared as children. It's important to always be open to learn from others and be willing to change your point of view when you get a better understanding.

I remember working with my students in the middle of the winter months at a high school in an underserved community in New Jersey. One morning it was freezing outside (20 degrees) and one of my students showed up to my home room shivering and he had no coat on. He was very small in stature for his age compared to his classmates. The only thing this student had on was a thin see through wind breaker. This student appeared mal- nourished and exhibited a distressed look on his face. I took him in private and asked him "where is your coat?" With a sad face he mumbled that he did not have one. I personally owned several winter coats which included a full-length fur coat. I immediately felt a responsibility as his teacher to help remedy his situation. In collaboration with the school social worker, my husband and I were able to purchase this young man a winter coat. I believe every human being need to spread kindness in every opportunity they have. Life is so unpredictable. I believe we are blessed when we are a blessing to others. I can attest to my life being so blessed and I believe it's because I have chosen to be laser focused in my decisions regarding others.

Ingredient 10

Leave A Legacy

What do you want people to say about you when you are no longer here?

As I begin to look over my life and the years I've spent as a wife, mother, grandmother, teacher, administrator, counselor, accomplished student, and a friend, I would hope that it would be said that I was a good person to all. By my husband being a pastor and a member of the clergy for many years, I have had many opportunities to attend funerals. Although some individuals were known not to be productive or upstanding in their community, I never heard a eulogy espouse anything but good things regarding their lives. Even when it was known by everyone that a particular individual lived a foul life, it was always stated at the funeral that he/she was an outstanding citizen or individual.

When it's time for me to transition into another life, I would hope that good things would be said but more importantly-that they are true.

Dr. O's 10 Essential Ingredients for Success   Marian Osborne, Ed D

As a wife I would hope that my husband of 50 years would say that he was confident that I loved him and that I treated him like a king. Many marriages don't last that long and still bear witness that there is much love and respect between the two. It wasn't hard for me to love and respect Reggie because he has always considered me first in everything he did. He is a kind and gentle man. He has never physically abused me, and he treats everyone with love unconditionally. He never failed to open the car door for me even during rainy days and after he had injured his leg and had to use a cane to walk. I never had to put gas in my car or take it to the car wash.

I want it to be said that I did return the same love and even more so when I took care of him when he was sick. He often tells the story how he was bed ridden in the hospital and was unable to wash himself after an operation of his right femur. This was early in our marriage. He marveled how I without hesitation was able to wash him in places he could not reach. The gentleman in the bed next to him did not experience the same from his significant other. He complained to Reggie how his wife said she couldn't do it. I want it to be said that I was a very good wife although never perfect.

Dr. O's 10 Essential Ingredients for Success   Marian Osborne, Ed D

As a mother, I would hope my daughters remember the love and care I gave them growing up even though I had no instructions on how to raise them. I would hope they would express how much I loved them and took good care of them as they matured into adulthood; and how I wanted them to be successful in life and I pushed them even when it didn't feel good to them. I want them to remember the importance of having good character and knowing that God put them here to be a blessing to others, including their family. I want them to say that I taught them the importance of loving God and making a commitment to obey what the Bible says.

As a grandmother, I want my three grandchildren to know for the rest of their lives that I have loved them unconditionally and that my prayer for them is that they would always depend on God. My husband and I have been blessed with two granddaughters and one grandson. Our eldest granddaughter is in her third year of college at the University of Connecticut. She is on an academic scholarship in the pharmacy school. Our grandson Earl Junior just began his academic scholarship program of engineering at Howard University. Our youngest granddaughter, Sydney or I call her my princess - is finishing her junior year in high school and has been inducted into the National Honor Society.

Although we are so proud of them, their journey has just begun. I want them to know they have inspired me to leave this book as a legacy to them. I want them to know that every hurdle I had to jump, every mountain I had to climb wasn't easy and I could not have made it without trusting God all the way. Proverbs 3:5-6 states *"Trust in the Lord with all thine heart; and lean not unto thine own understanding. In all thy ways acknowledge Him, and He shall direct thy paths"*.

As a teacher, I would hope that my students remember my kindness and encouragement. As a teacher I realize that children who are having difficulty in school often have the same dreams about the future as those students experiencing success in school. Unfortunately, they too often receive less encouragement in school, and are often part of a select school community that feels inferior academically and socially. I would hope that my students would say that they remember me as helping them develop high self-esteem and competency skills that they so desperately needed. I would hope they would say I went over and above my responsibilities as a teacher to assist them when they needed it the most. I hope they will remember that I visited their homes and met their parents to ensure the best in their educational lives.

As an administrator, I would hope that my staff remembered me in a most professional way. I would like them to say that I was deliberate in guiding them with principles that lead to inner thought and outward behavior, resulting in personal as well as professional integrity. I hope they felt I helped in moving them beyond mere success. I would like them to say that I energized them through modeling a level of professionalism. I want them to say that Dr. Marian Osborne had a profound influence on their life and assisted them in capitulating strategies that will be with them the rest of their life.

As a counselor I would hope my counselees

would say I helped them grow in knowledge, skills and attitudes regarding their recovery. I would like them to say that I was non-judgmental while using strategies to enhance their process for recovery. I can remember when I realized that I needed to change my own attitude towards individuals in recovery. Having been brought up in a strict religious household I was taught that people who took drugs made a decision to do so and therefore were evil people. They were not Godly, and they had no intentions of doing the right thing. I was taught that they were just bad people.

After educating myself on addiction, I had a paradigm shift. I began to realize that no one is perfect. All have sinned and fall short of the glory of God. (Romans 3:23 NIV) Just because I was raised in the church and lived what society call a pretty good life, no one is perfect in God's sight. People need people. If I was fortunate to have someone teach me growing up, then it's my responsibility to teach and love others in this world. I would hope that my counselees were able to see an appreciation I had for them just being who they are.

As a sister, I would like my siblings to say that they loved me for who I am. As I begin to write about my siblings, I can't stop the tears from flowing down my face because my beloved brother died within the past two weeks. I have had many opportunities to reflect on my relationship with him these past weeks. If my brother could speak now, I believe he would say I was a good sister to him. I believe he would say that I loved him and demonstrated my love for him in many instances. He would say when he came to Florida from Brooklyn, New York, to visit my husband and me, that we took exceptional care of him. My brother had asthma and congestive heart issues his entire life and walking great distances was difficult for him. There were times my husband and I would pay for a limousine service for him in order for him to attend a family event. He would say that he felt special but never wanted to be a burden. Although my three sisters and I had misunderstandings during our life time, I am confident that they know that I love them deeply. Family is very important to me and I hold each one in high regard.

As a student, I was able to maintain all A's and one B+ throughout my entire post graduate work at Seton Hall University. I would hope that my professors would say that I worked diligently in order to graduate on time, with honors. I was always looking and searching for information and knowledge. I had a hunger to learn and be productive.

As a friend, I want to be remembered as someone who was honest. I have learned in life that being honest doesn't always bring friends your way. It will weed out those people you don't need in your life. Genuine friendship is giving of you to someone without looking for something in return. Real friendship is when someone knows everything about someone else whether good or bad and you are still their friend.

In conclusion, people can have success in life in spite of their experiences. Everyone will encounter problems in their life. Sometimes they are predictable but other times they are not. Traumatic experiences can begin during childhood and/or throughout adulthood. It can be the sudden death of a child or a parent, an unfulfilled relationship, a disappointment of a promise, inadequate health care that leads to a fatality, lack of job opportunities, years of inadequate education, racism perpetrated towards the group you belong to, civil unrest, or even the lack of family structure in your life.

The important question I had to ask myself and you must do the same is - what do you do when faced with these hardships. How do you move forward when plagued with so many issues? I have personally learned over the years that the only way I was able to maintain my resilience and strength was that I had to constantly build on it. I had to constantly develop an "I can do it attitude" When doors of opportunities seemed to close, I remembered that one door that closes leaves ten open just for me. I knew in my heart that God was always giving me chances to move forward in life. I stayed positive no matter what life brought my way. I know this sounds easier said than done but believe me it's possible.

Having had a spiritual experience with God, I was able to accomplish so much. Through meditation and prayer, I was able to release the stress. I learned bible phrases that increased my faith that gave me an assurance that I was not by myself. I learned to walk in love and forgiveness. I tried to keep my heart tender and speak words of hope and victory over myself. Unfortunately, we all don't start from the same place. Problems seem to be multiplied among those who are underserved in our communities. As a result, they often don't have the family support that is needed.

Traumatic experiences do vary and therefore those individuals who find that they are drowning must seek out help. Sometimes that help might come from ongoing counseling, from a supportive church family, a mentor, or just dedicated friends with knowledge of what your needs are. Whatever difficulties we encounter in life, we must know that there is always someone out there to help us through our difficult times. We must make every effort to look in places where we can find that someone. There are so many good people in this world and I want to be remembered as one who was willing to lend a hand to help and speak words of hope and victory over myself.

Doctoral Graduation – 1999
Education Administration
Dr. Marian Osborne

The Gallery

The Crew Family

Barbara, Marian, Philip, Mother Crew, Linda & Theresa

Sisters

Mother & Daughters

Dana – Marian's favorite cousin

Dr. O's 10 Essential Ingredients for Success   Marian Osborne, Ed D

Grandson Earl

Granddaughter Sydney

Granddaughter Jasmine

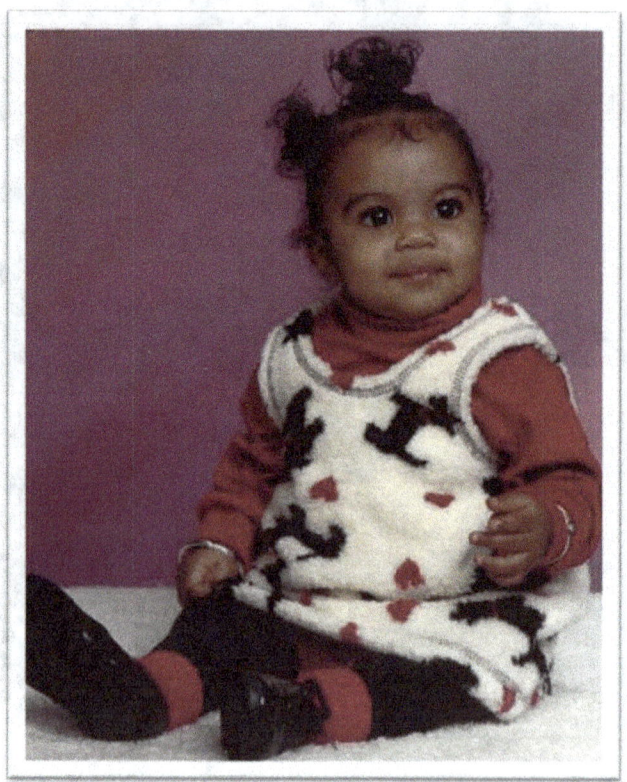

Dr. O's 10 Essential Ingredients for Success   Marian Osborne, Ed D

Marian in Hawaii on vacation

Dr. O's 10 Essential Ingredients for Success   Marian Osborne, Ed D

Reggie in Hawaii on Vacation

Marian

Master's Degree graduation

www.ingramcontent.com/pod-product-compliance
Lightning Source LLC
Chambersburg PA
CBHW070108120526
44588CB00032B/1377